Gunpowder, Apples and Cement

Gunpowder, Apples and Cement

Published by The Conrad Press in the United Kingdom 2020

Tel: +44(0)1227 472 874
www.theconradpress.com
info@theconradpress.com

ISBN 978-1-913567-24-8

Typesetting and Cover Design by:
Charlotte Mouncey, www.bookstyle.co.uk

The Conrad Press logo was designed by Maria Priestley.

Printed and bound in Great Britain by Clays Ltd, Elcograf S.p.A.

Gunpowder, Apples and Cement

The story of an English country home

Evelyn Cook

'Historical buildings do not belong to us only. They belonged to our forefathers and they will belong to our descendants, unless we play them false. They are not in any sense our property to do as we like with them. We are only trustees for those who come after us.'

William Morris

Opening address to the 12th Annual Meeting of the Society for the Protection of Ancient Buildings, 1889

Acknowledgments:

Although much of the research, and all of the errors and assumptions, are my own, I owe thanks to the following for their help with this book.

Dr James Gibson of the Rochester Bridge Trust, who gave permission for me to consult the Trust archives about Vitale de Michele's tenure as Bridge Engineer; Dr Malcolm Underwood, then Archivist at St John's College Cambridge, who found the auction catalogue extract from 1843 which provided the link to Edward Eagleton's ownership; the staff of Kent and Medway Local History Archives who provided access to the County Archives; the late Professor C J Holdsworth, whose kind testimonial gained me access to the de Michele papers in the Bodleian Library which contributed significantly to this book; the late Rupert Lascelles, Max Batchelor, Matthew (Pelham) Smithers and Deirdre Catmur who shared their memories of the house with me; and Fr Andrew Davis, who very kindly gave me access to his unpublished thesis on Higham Priory.

Most of all my thanks go to my husband Martin and my children - for accommodating my longing to live in a historic house, and putting up with the very long gestation period of this book. Martin in particular has helped me enormously with editing and proof reading, and constructive comments - but more than anything, by giving me encouragement to believe that I was writing something worthwhile, rather than simply a self-indulgence.

Evelyn Cook
Whitstable, Kent
June 2020

Contents

Introduction

This is Higham Hall - our home for five years between 2010 and 2015, and the subject of this book. When you live in an old house, you become very conscious that other people have been here before you - and those people have made decisions about the house and its rooms, planned and tended gardens and brought up families in the home you have made. Any old house becomes almost a shared home, with a history developed over many years. And, as Bill Bryson said, you become aware of how much national history informs this most local of histories:

*'Whatever happens in the world - whatever is discovered
or created or bitterly fought over- eventually ends up, in
one way or another, in your house. Wars, famine, the
Industrial Revolution, the Enlightenment - they are all
there in your sofas and chests of drawers, tucked inside the
folds of your curtains… in the paint on your walls and
the water in your pipes. So the history of household life
isn't just a history of beds and sofas and kitchen stoves…
but of scurvy and guano and the Eiffel Tower and bedbugs
and bodysnatching and just about everything else that has
ever happened. Houses aren't refuges from history. They are
where history ends up.'* [1]

Taking this as its theme, this study is an attempt to throw
some light on the varied inhabitants of one such house in the
village of Higham in Kent, and to see how one group of people,
linked by a common house, played a role in and were shaped
by local and national events.

Higham is equidistant between Rochester and Gravesend
and originally on the edge of the marshes which Dickens
eloquently describes in 'Great Expectations':

*' …that… dark flat wilderness beyond the churchyard,
intersected with dykes and mounds and gates, with scattered cattle feeding on it, was the marshes; and that low
leaden line beyond, was the river; and the distant savage
lair from which the wind was rushing, was the sea…where
our village lay, on the flat in-shore among the alder trees
and pollards, a mile or more from the church…'* [2]

Higham is not a normal picturesque Wealden Kent village,

but the pattern of settlement of the village makes its history all the more interesting. A village in three parts, Higham neatly illustrates the development of local transport and the changing focus of the community it served. The original Higham, with its Norman Church and twelfth-century priory, was located beside the Thames marshes, on the southern end of the Higham to East Tilbury ferry route. During the medieval period and later, more substantial roads developed for carts and coaches - but these were built on the higher, drier ground to the south of the original village, with inns such as the Falstaff at Gads Hill serving the travelling public.

Gradually, the lure of the road drew some settlement away from the river, but this was on the basis of scattered hamlets and homesteads built during the late medieval and early modern periods, between the original Higham (now known as Church Street) and Gad's Hill - with Higham Hall, Mockbeggar and Green Lane Farm being the most prominent settlements. However, in this period, there is no evidence of the sprawling long village of Higham joining up Church Street and Gads Hill as it does now, and the two places would have remained separate hamlets. The Chequers, an inn dating from the eighteenth century in the Church Street area had few neighbours apart from a nearby forge.[3]

It was the coming of the canal, and then the railway which replaced it, which led to infilling and the development of Victorian - now Lower - Higham. This new link provided a very efficient route to Gravesend to the west and the Medway Towns to the east. Lower Higham began as a collection of workers cottages around the station in the mid nineteenth century and gradually spread southwards up the hill (originally called Higham Hill Lane) towards the High Road. As it grew, the modern village centre was referred to as 'Higham Upshire', or latterly 'mid-Higham' (as the post office was called until very recently). Here a new church was built in the nineteenth century to serve the migrated and expanded population and a grand vicarage was built at the railway end of the village, subsequently turned into a private house and named 'The Knowle'.

Undoubtedly Higham's most famous resident was Charles Dickens. By his time, the village was a more unified whole, with houses dotted along Telegraph Hill and several farms occupying the land between the railway and the Gravesend to Rochester High Road. It was still by no means urban - Mary (Mamie) Dickens in her memoir '*My Father as I recall him*' refers to '*our little country station, Higham*', describing a journey from London back to Gads Hill.[4]

The twentieth century changed the nature of Higham, as populations and road traffic increased, and towns like Gravesend required a 'commuter belt'. Council and private housing replaced the fields and orchards around the village.

Today the focus of Higham is still somewhat split, between the A226 and Dicken's home (now a school) where the Tour de France passed through the village in 2007, and the Olympic Torch relay ran in 2012, and the recreation ground and memorial hall lower down the hill, where regular events take place throughout the year. The station, busy with Thameslink commuters to London, Gravesend and Dartford is now on the northern fringe of the village in Lower Higham. The old marsh church where Higham began is unused for all but three or four special events a year.

Yet it is still possible to gain some impression of the old Higham. Walking the old causeway out to the river shore, a degree of imagination is required to ignore the gravel works and the looming cranes of the Thames Gateway container port. But sheep still graze the marshes in summer. And watching the stately progress of container ships up and down the estuary, you can imagine a time when the focus of the village was still directed northwards, towards the river. Barges carried grain, fruit and latterly cement to London along the Thames. Then, as now, the boats tower over a person standing on the marsh. They seem to traverse the fields. With a little more imagination, you can stand on the slope of the hill leading up to Higham, by the end of Walmer Avenue, and imagine the river teeming with red sailed Thames barges carrying bricks into London, sailing clippers bringing tea to the East India docks or, more fancifully perhaps, one or two of the wooden warships built at Deptford or Woolwich, sailing down to anchor in the Medway.

Higham's history has been shaped by the river, and one of the many features of Higham Hall is the distant view of ships from the top floor windows, and the sound of fog horns on a misty night, or on New Year's Eve. Much of my adult life has been spent living near the Thames and its estuary, and it has been a fascinating exercise to learn more about one of the villages which grew up on the banks of the 'dirty old river', and to realise how much history there can be in a seemingly ordinary place.[5]

Higham Hall

The rather grand title of our former house - Higham Hall - is a little misleading. When we first noticed the name on a local map (we lived in the converted stables of Mockbeggar House at the time), I spent some time looking for a grand mansion, and was initially disappointed to find only a square looking tower visible from the side, in Taylor's Lane - itself a small, steep and rather uninviting country lane with high banked sides. Driving past the house, you notice some old and very high garden walls and, until recently, a magnificent and ancient wisteria was visible for two or three weeks in the spring. However, the house itself seemed quite nondescript.

A few years later the house came up for sale, and although it was clearly a nonsensical move in economic terms (our children were almost grown with two of them away at University), curiosity won out and we looked around the house with its impressive name and listed garden walls. I, at least, decided it was THE house I had always wanted to live in, and - supportive as they always have been - my family accepted the idea - despite the disruption caused to my husband's plans for retirement!

We bought Higham Hall in September 2010, and it was simply wonderful to live there, even with the need for repairs to its listed fabric and the ongoing cost of running a large house and gardens. It is a family home and a welcoming one, and one of the most rewarding things about living there was the opportunity to find out something about the people who came before us. The house has reflected some of the social change which has taken place in the South East of England. It is not a grand house; rather it has been a house for people making their way in life - for the middle classes indeed - and one with a solid tradition of hard work behind its wealth, rather than inheritance. Over the 350 years that records go back, the house has been home to army officers, tenant farmers, clockmakers, lawyers and magistrates, professionals and entrepreneurs, as well as a civil engineer and cement maker of note and a seventeenth-century gunpowder maker. From the late nineteenth century to the Second World War, the house enjoyed the status of one of Higham's 'big houses', with its tree lined drive into School Lane, and a seventy acre fruit farm attached to it. Since then, it has retreated into being a more private house, in keeping with its humbler origins. But it retains its history and that of its owners and occupiers, and it has been a real pleasure researching and putting this book together.

The book begins with a look at the history of Higham village, and I then make some suggestions as to the origins of the house, and the ownership of the land on which it was built, before concentrating on the stories of the families who are known to have lived at Higham Hall. I discuss the physical shape of the house only in the context of those families - as befits a house with a 400 year history as a family home.

Chapter 1

Higham - a North Kent village

'The Parish of Higham, is situated on the north side of the high London Road, nearly opposite to Shorne. It lies low, adjoining the marshes, the river Thames being its northern boundary. The air of this district is extremely unhealthy, tending to produce intermittents, a fatality which appends in general to those parishes lying on the north side of the high road... The surface is flat and the soil in general very fertile... The village and church stand close to and exposed to the marshes, which comprise nearly half the parish.'

Writing in 1829, William Ireland makes the location sound rather unattractive.[5] In researching any house history, the first question is who built it and why. In the case of Higham Hall, why did a substantial farmhouse end up in what appears today to be a fairly unpropitious area of North Kent marshland? The dating of the house and the garden walls (see page 32) suggests that before the current house itself was built, there was probably some kind of small estate or holding - even if that only covered the extent of the farmstead and one or two fields around it. But why did that develop there, as an agricultural unit, with or without a dwelling house? The answer is a combination of many factors and requires a brief examination of why Higham itself arose as a populated settlement.

Looking back to the pre-Iron Age era - roughly before 1200 BCE - Peter Drewett (writing in the Longman Regional History of England series) suggests that the Thames Estuary was an area of seasonal, low density occupation. [6] Nomadic peoples used the river as a source of food (mostly shellfish) and will only have spent the spring and summer periods in the area, as it became marshy and unpleasant in the winter months.

As the development of iron tools encouraged small scale agriculture, it is likely that small settlements grew up a little distance from the edges of the river - and even now, it is not difficult to imagine small groups of settlers wanting to live on the drier, higher and wooded pieces of land alongside the Thames, using the marshes to collect shellfish and salt. A F Allen recorded the finding of Roman rubbish pits, pottery, charcoal and graves, dating from the fourth century BCE, in the Shorne and East Chalk areas[7].

The Roman invasion in the first century CE caused significant population expansion in the south-east, leading to the settlement of previously under-utilised land as shown by the significant archaeological finds from this period in the area of the Thames Estuary. [8] In particular, substantial pottery remains have been found in the area of Cliffe Pools, suggesting that the pools were originally dug out for their clay during the whole three centuries of the Roman occupation. English Heritage have suggested that pottery remains found in Higham saltings (bordering the Thames) are evidence of Roman settlement.

Of particular interest to historians of Higham has been the purpose of an old causeway, which can still be traced across the marshes. [9] This raised track runs from the Thames and

19

off towards Denton, with a branch diverting back towards St Mary's church. Hasted describes an ancient ferry, which he considers was

'[probably] a frequented ford or passage in the time of the Romans, [because of] the visible remains of the raised causeway, or road, near thirty feet wide, leading from the Thames side through the marshes by Higham'

He wrote that the ford was 'said to have been' crossed by Plautius during Claudius' invasion of Britain in 43 CE, adding :

'Between [Higham and East Tilbury] there was a ferry on the river for many ages after, the method of intercourse between the two counties of Kent and Essex for all these parts, and it continued so till the dissolution of the abbey here; before which time, Higham was likewise the place for shipping and unshipping corn and goods in great quantities from this part of the county to and from London and elsewhere.' [10]

His sources here are local antiquarians, but a cursory glance at the map confirms that this remains one of the narrowest stretches of the river in the immediate area even today. The ability to cross the water with some ease is confirmed by the Domesday Survey (see page 23). Roach Smith, writing in 1880 refers to a wealth of Roman Pottery and tiles being found in the churchyard of St Mary, Higham, near to the beginning of the causeway. [11]

This archaeological evidence makes it reasonable to conclude that there were settlements in Higham in the Roman period and it is at least probable that the ferry crossing Hasted refers to dates from pre-Roman times. In 1934, the Higham school-master, Captain Steadman elaborated on the ferry in a talk to villagers. He described the causeway as a raised and paved track to the river and *'one of the most ancient routes in Europe…used by Phoenician tin miners…[for which] proof [was] found in caches of tin dropped in transit'*, before describing how the river could be forded at this point, until the cutting of channels for ships required the establishment of a ferry.

More recent research suggests Captain Steadman's rather grandiose claims for the Higham crossing were exaggerated, although it is likely that it was a useful and well-established route in Roman times. [12] We need to look north west of Higham, to Springhead and the Ebbsfleet Valley to explain its purpose. Work on the Channel Tunnel Rail Link in the late 1990s confirmed that Springhead was a site of great religious importance in both Roman Britain and in earlier centuries. Finds from 300 BCE to 150 CE have been discovered in this area, with its main development taking place between the first and fourth centuries CE. Archaeologists believe the Celts began settling the site of the Ebbsfleet valley around 100 BCE, drawn to the area by the spiritual significance they attached to the eight natural springs which rise to form the river. When the Romans invaded, Springhead turned into a Roman supply base and settlement, but retained its spiritual significance, with as many as a dozen temples established there during the late first century CE. [13]

This settlement at Springhead (called Vagniacis by the Romans) lay squarely on Watling Street, the Ebbsfleet River providing a link from there to the Thames. A waterfront town was established on the banks of the Ebbsfleet from the second to the fourth century. A direct line can be traced from Higham causeway, through Gravesend, to the River Ebbsfleet and then on to Springhead, suggesting that there was some kind of link between the settlements at Higham and Springhead - perhaps for the supply of pottery or shellfish, or more imaginatively, to cross to Essex. [14] In a desk based assessment of the Cliffe Pools area, Richard James points to studies that show sea levels were three metres lower during the Roman period and that land which is now marsh would have been dry land, which could have supported pottery manufacture and trade, using the naturally occurring clay and the transport facilities offered by the river. [15]

With this in mind, we should see Higham as a place of some significance (albeit small). With links to Springhead and across the Thames, as well as pottery manufacture either on site or nearby (Cliffe), the village was favourably sited in a well settled area. To the east, Rochester developed into an important Roman centre and port, perhaps with responsibility for the western part of Kent. [16]

After the departure of the Romans, much of Kent was settled by Germanic peoples who were leaving the newly inundated areas of Frisia (in the Netherlands) and Northern Germany in search of drier land, but land which was similar in nature to the places they had left. [17] The Thames Estuary was a popular place for these settlements, and the suffix 'ham' in Higham (meaning settlement or high place hemmed in by water, or marsh) is itself evidence of Anglo-Saxon settlement. [18]

By the end of the fifth century CE, Kent had emerged as a relatively stable Anglo-Saxon Kingdom and it is likely that settlements by the Thames continued to make use of the shellfish, fish and salt available in the estuary, to supplement the meat and arable crops raised on drained land.[19] Willows grown on the marshes were used to make fish traps in the river. While there is no evidence of significant population density in this area between the fifth and tenth centuries, it seems likely that the settlements did not die out. Rather they continued a low-key existence in the shadow of much larger settlements such as Rochester, and Cliffe - which developed into a notable Saxon town after the eighth century - yet maintaining their usefulness as a place where travellers and traders could cross the river by ferry.

As late as the eleventh century the Domesday survey lends support to the notion that there were frequent crossings at Higham between Kent and Essex, referring to land for 200 sheep in Essex belonging to Higham manor. Even with our 'improved' transport links, a farmer of today would think twice about having his sheep pastured over the river, which perhaps gives us a false perspective of the separation between these two counties in earlier times. While today we orientate Higham southwards focusing on the Gravesend to Rochester Road, for much of the village's early history it's face was towards the river Thames which provided its principal transport routes, and thus northwards to Essex.

It is worth noting at this point that a distinct system of landholding developed in Kent in the pre-Norman Conquest period. Gavelkind was quite different from the method of land-holding more widely employed in England - that of customary tenure which gave rights over sale and inheritance to the lord of the manor. Gavelkind was a form of partible inheritance whereby land could be passed on to a number of heirs, and could be alienated at will, without depending on the permission of the senior tenant (the 'lord' of the manor, or other freeholder). This not only encouraged the development of small, and thus affordable holdings, it allowed for the buying and selling of land, and for those wealthy enough to buy, the consolidation of small, manageable estates.[20]

Gavelkind will come up subsequently as an issue in this history, but for our immediate purposes, it operated as a positive factor in the development of a commercial market in land and of consolidated landholding in Kent. This continued after the Norman Conquest. After their prompt submission to Duke William at Dover in 1066, the men of Kent were permitted to keep their customary gavelkind and its distinctive form encouraged the development of small settlements and farmsteads dispersed throughout the county.

Peter Brandon and Brian Short highlight the fertility of the band of brickearth loam which skirts this area of the North Kent Coast.[21] As agriculture developed, this type of land was used for a combination of sheep and corn farming, with farmers using the rich marshland pastureland for grazing in the summer and moving sheep to manure the arable land in the winter. The salt on the marshes protected the sheep from many common foot diseases and long fallow periods on the land could be avoided by this natural application of manure.[22] In this way, over the centuries, corn production improved sufficiently to generate a surplus. The cycle was elaborated in the thirteenth century with the introduction of beans and legumes for fodder crops. This rotation is still evident today - you can see that some of the fields around Higham used for wheat in the summer will be planted with a fast growing fodder crop after harvest, before sheep are turned out on it to clear and manure the land. Then the sheep are moved back on to the marshland for the next arable crop to be sown.

Sea levels rose during the twelfth century and the marshland remained subject to frequent inundations throughout the fourteenth and fifteenth centuries. There was some enclosure by banks, but these were not sufficiently robust to keep out the river. However, throughout the medieval period, the marshes were used whenever they could be and there was merit in preserving the saltiness of the land, for the health of the sheep. At the same time, use of the higher land for arable crops continued, as is demonstrated by the construction of large barns for crop storage, such as the 210 foot long tithe barn which (just) survives at Frindsbury, near Strood.[23] It is worth noting that the land at Higham Hall echoes this local pattern. From the seventeenth to the twentieth century, the farm estate consisted of a farmstead with a large barn, outlying arable fields (later orchards) and small areas of saltings closer to the river.

The early use of a manuring cycle supported surplus production. Arable crops, such as wheat and rye, were sold, rather than supporting the local manor or being used for subsistence farming. As early as the late Saxon period, the frequency of town mints (Hythe, Dover, Canterbury, Sandwich, Old Romney, Dover and Rochester) suggests that trade was comparatively extensive in Kent, and thirteenth-century evidence from Faversham shows that surplus corn was sold through the port to London. The presence of a ready market for goods encouraged improvements such as the introduction of regular manuring cycles (see above), and Brandon and Short highlight how the prosperity of the Hoo and Gravesham areas rose from fourth (out of the six areas of North Kent) in the fourteenth century, to first out of six in the sixteenth century, as a result of these efficiencies. [24] Crop rotation supported the growing of wheat for the London market.

As we have already noted, as road transport improved, the road between Gravesend and Rochester formed an increasingly important role in the village. Of necessity, horses, carts and carriages had always used the drier land to the south, and this route became a part of the pilgrimage and cross channel traffic to Rochester, Canterbury and Dover. Rebuilt in the fourteenth century, the old Roman bridge at Rochester was the only way to cross the Medway river apart from Maidstone, some twenty miles south. Gravesend was the starting place for the Long Ferry to London. Established by charter in 1401, the Long Ferry offered a safe, three-hour journey to London on a favourable tide. This area above Higham (known as Gad's Hill then and now) was still a relatively uninhabited area and there were frequent attacks by highwaymen and footpads, well known enough to have been used as a comic device in Shakespeare's Henry IV, Part One. One scene refers to pilgrims travelling to the shrine at Canterbury (written in the late sixteenth century, the reference is to the tomb of Thomas Beckett) with *'rich offerings'* and *'traders riding to London with fat purses'* [25].

In the sixteenth century, Lambarde describes the area as *'wealthy'* with the yeoman *'nowhere more free and jolly than in this shyre (sic)'* [26]. Ann Brown, on the other hand, argues that the area did not become prosperous before the development of fruit growing in the sixteenth and seventeenth centuries, although she does highlight the intrinsic value of the land in this area, which resulted from its proximity to London and position (almost) as a commuter belt.[27] In her article, '*London and North West Kent in the later middle ages: the development of a land market*', she argues that changing social conditions in the fourteenth and fifteenth centuries encouraged rich gentry to escape the pressures and risks to health of London life by investing in '*a tranquil residence*' out of town. She suggests that although the soil was poor, the proximity of great ecclesiastical foundations (Canterbury and Rochester), as well as the favourable system of land tenure encouraged rich gentry to buy land in the area. Lambarde himself gives evidence of this, describing '*courtiers, lawyers, and merchants [who] be continually translated and become new plants among them.*'[28] Then, as now, any piece of land unencumbered by inheritance rights or a life interest represented a good investment for those with rising amounts of cash earned from trade but with little or no inherited land of their own.

Timber framed houses (using wood from the extensive forests in the Weald) were built in Kent from late Middle Ages onwards and the area developed into the familiar landscape of scattered farmsteads we still see today. The local homesteads of Filborough Farm (nearer to Chalk, Filborough dates from at least the seventeenth century), Green Farm, Mockbeggar and Higham Hall typify this pattern of development. Higham Hall, though not itself the classic timber framed Wealden hall house often found in Kent, is a good example of the type of courtyard farmstead built during the sixteenth and seventeenth centuries in lowland farming areas.[29]

During this period, the diversity of agricultural production in the North Kent area increased. Fruit, previously imported from the Low Countries, (such as strawberries, raspberries, currants and gooseberries) was now grown commercially for sale. Farmers still used the marshland for their stock, enabling the drier areas to be ploughed for cereals and also planted fruit trees, vegetables and hops (although the capital investment required for hop growing meant that it was not a popular crop for small landholders). Gravesend became a prosperous market gardening area and contemporary documents are full of references to smallholders and tenants described as 'gardeners'. Pehr Kalm, a Finnish botanist visiting the area in 1748 remarked on the delightful countryside

> '...with earth walls along the Thames protecting the farmland at high tide; haystacks of sanfoin [a perennial legume used in place of hay]; and large areas of wheat... A little rye... together with buckwheat and luxuriant crops of tares [vetch - a fodder crop] were grown, while beans and peas were sown in rows. And between Gravesend and Rochester, were many cherry orchards sending fruit by the boatload to London.'[30]

Land use continued in this pattern until the mid-nineteenth century, when the amount and productivity of usable land could not keep pace with the growth in population. Taking advantage of the growth in rail and canal transport, London and other South East towns began to rely on a wider network for food production. At the same time, industry began to make greater use of the Thames and Medway rivers and the areas alongside them. Cement works grew up between Dartford and Gravesend, paper manufacture in Dartford and brick and gunpowder manufacture south of the Isle of Sheppey. As we will see, local industries had as much influence on Higham Hall in its later years as its attraction as an agricultural investment had on the beginnings of the estate.

By the 1830s and 1840s, Gravesend had developed into a combined port and watering place, with Rosherville Gardens and Windmill Hill attracting day visitors from London. The surrounding villages continued to produce large quantities of vegetables (peas and turnips) and wheat, to be shipped to London. By 1839, the railway was extended through Higham to the Medway Towns, enabling daily contact with London and facilitating the movement of perishable goods, as well as people.

1830 to 1900 was probably the heyday of industrial production in the area. The cement industry wound down early in the twentieth century, with many works closing, although paper making continued to flourish, After 1900, agricultural production also experienced more difficulty - increased competition from America had adversely affected arable production after the 1870s and increasing imports of French and Belgian fruit in the early twentieth century made fruit farming less profitable.

The nadir of agricultural production was the inter-war period - in 1934, for example, wheat prices were at their lowest since 1771.[31] This decline prompted widespread changes in the use of both farmland and farmhouses throughout the South East, with old houses becoming divorced from the land that previously supported them, and kitchen gardens and orchards turned into gardens and paddocks. The houses became prized for their peaceful and rural setting, rather than for the productive land that came with them. Whilst Higham Hall managed to stave off this fate until after the Second World War, there is evidence that it was no longer paying its way by the 1920s, and its role as the hub of a small agricultural estate gradually dwindled.

The late nineteenth and early twentieth centuries also saw a significant move away from the land by the rural workforce in the North Kent area. Here, competition for labour from the Strood Brickworks and Chatham Dockyard pushed up wages and attracted younger men into manufacturing, while the average age of the agricultural workforce increased. The use of women on the land during the War years is noted by one of our owners, and the years 1905-1945 show a significant shift in the position of women at Higham Hall as landowners and managers. Finally, the later chapters of this book demonstrate the trend criticised by both William Cobbett and John Ruskin, who bemoaned the translation of farmhouses into homes '*with carpeted parlours and a bell push*', decrying the effect on land prices which increased farmers' difficulties.[32]

As Brandon and Short say,

> '*the village has survived architecturally, but not socially. The 'new countrymen' are persons whose livelihood is made in the towns but who commute to rural peace in the evenings or at weekends.*'[33]

Certainly, for the last seventy years of its history, Higham Hall has had no connection with agricultural production, beyond its situation in the middle of working farmland. This can lead to misunderstandings of the history of the house. As we will see, the house has been a farmhouse for more than three quarters of its 400 year history, and only gentrified over the last 100 years or so.

Having summarised the local context, I now turn to look in more detail at the location of Higham Hall itself, and how the building of the house reflected some national historical trends.

Chapter 2

Early ownership

Having summarised the agricultural and economic context of North Kent, we need to look a little more closely at Higham, and its geographical position. An important feature, bringing notice if not prosperity to Higham, was its situation on the Dover-Rochester-London route. The origins of today's A2 trunk road lie along Watling Street, developed from Roman times, but it is worth remembering that the current A2 route, south of Shorne Woods and Gravesend, only dates from around 1924. As we have seen today's A226, through Higham Upshire, was the major route from Rochester to Gravesend, and thence to London. The popularity of this road route led to it being the first turnpiked road in Kent in 1711 (i.e. tolls were collected for its upkeep). An evocative passage in Andrew Roote's *'History of Higham, Volume 1'* reads:

> *'By the time Victoria came to the throne in 1837 the main road through Higham was very busy. The author Eliza Lynn Linton, who used to live at Gad's Hill Place in the 1830s recalled of the highway then: 'It was as gay as an approach to a metropolis. Ninety-two public coaches and pleasure vans used to pass in a day, not counting the private carriages of the grandees posting luxuriously to Dover for*

Paris and the Grand Tour. Soldiers marching or riding to or from Chatham and Gravesend to embark for India or on their return journey home; ship's companies paid off that morning and cruising past the gates, shouting and singing and comporting themselves in a generally terrifying manner... '[34]

It needs to be kept in mind throughout this study, therefore, that, at least until the early twentieth century, Higham's location made it a place that many travellers would pass through, rather than it being the quiet suburban village that it is today. This makes the fact that quite significant people have lived at Higham Hall a little easier to understand.

The current English Heritage listing for Higham Hall house and it's garden walls says:

'Higham Hall, 18th C front with earlier sixteenth or seventeenth-century structure inside. Modern extension to west and north. Red brick. Tiled roof. Two storeys with three storeys to west. Sash windows with glazing bars and hipped dormers. 18th C doorway in splayed angle of west end with flat hood pilasters and 6 panel door. 18th century chimney pieces and doorcases internally.

Gardens to north and south of house enclosed with 10ft high walls of sixteenth century brick in English bond. Buttresses at regular intervals. Two beeboles in west wall of south court but this has been demolished in part to allow a drive to the front door. Arched recesses in east and west walls of north court. (21 November 1966)* '[35]

The picture below illustrates both the beeboles (alcoves for wicker beehives) and the gap in the west wall.

Fig 1 : the West Garden Wall at Higham Hall

How did it come about that this sixteenth or seventeenth-century house was built in Higham, and who by? To answer this, we need to look first at who might originally have owned the land it stood upon.

Our earliest comprehensive source of land ownership is the Domesday Book. Before the Norman Conquest there was no such system for landownership in Britain and certainly no complete evidential source for who held or occupied particular tracts of land. Although various tracts of land might be held by Charter from the King (not always the King of all of England in the pre-Conquest period), there were significant and numerous pieces of unclaimed land. The Normans introduced the concept of landholding still in use today: that all land is ultimately owned by, and held from, the Crown.

In practice, this freehold tenure from the Crown now confers no additional demands on the freeholder beyond the understanding that their ownership is limited in terms of the space over and under their land, and in some cases, in terms of the mineral rights of that land. But at the time it was a significant and material change in establishing a unified system of landholding with its accompanying duties to the Crown and any superior landlord.

From the Conquest onwards, therefore, it is right to begin looking at the question of who owned the land of a particular estate or household, although that can be very difficult to establish with certainty for small pieces of land, like the Higham Hall estate. And as we will see, from surviving characteristics, the existing house appears to date from the period of the 'Great Rebuilding' in the late sixteenth and early seventeenth centuries (see page 55), so no conclusions can readily be drawn regarding whether 'this' Higham Hall is the first dwelling on the site, or whether an older, more modest dwelling was there for many years before.

The Domesday Book (1086) lists a church and a mill in Higham, and notes that Higham comprised two manors - Higham and Lillechurch. Domesday includes the whole village amongst those lands (in common with much of Kent) given by William I to his half brother, Bishop Odo of Bayeux. Following Odo's rebellion against William Rufus in 1088 his lands were confiscated, and returned to the possessions of the Crown, from whence it becomes more difficult to trace their head ownership, although the local tenants in occupation would not have been immediately affected by this change.

So with this context in mind, who were the early owners of the land which became Higham Hall, and why did they settle there in particular? There are two obvious candidates - a Priory founded in the twelfth century by King Stephen and Queen Matilda, and the dominant local family, the Cobham/Brookes. The land owned by Odo of Bayuex, William I's half-brother, comprised Higham and Lillechurch manors, together with Merston, Beckley and Chalk. Shorne was not listed as a separate manor. In other local records, by the fifteenth and sixteenth centuries, Merston and Beckley manors had disappeared, the manors of Randall and Shorne have been added, and Lillechurch manor has been subsumed into Higham. At this later point in time, the major landowners were Higham priory (and subsequently St John's College Cambridge) and the (de) Cobham family.

Higham Priory

Higham Priory, founded around 1148 by King Stephen and Queen Matilda was built on the edge of Higham marshes, close to the ferry crossing. The background to this royal foundation in Higham is set out later in this chapter, but it was assumed by previous owners of Higham Hall and local historians that the Higham Hall estate had a connection with the priory. These tentative conclusions were that the estate may have been a farmstead that grew up around a barn originally belonging to the priory. Perhaps it might have been a grange* for arable lands cultivated some two miles from the priory itself. Perhaps the house originated as the home of a steward or bailiff, or perhaps the fields were rented to a tenant who subsequently built himself a farmhouse among his fields? One fanciful story, quoted in 'A Handbook of Higham',[36] is that a tunnel ran from under Higham Hall to the priory itself. The fact that such a tunnel would need to run for a mile and a half under land which is often extremely wet, and that no discernible purpose would be served by it, discredits the story. Certainly no trace of it has ever been found despite various buildings being erected along its potential route.

My view is that, while superficially plausible, attempts to link the house to the priory are simply efforts to use a known feature (the priory) to try to explain a rather more puzzling one - the existence of an ancient house and estate which has no apparent logic to its position. An examination of the history of the Priory lands, and those of the Cobham estates, suggests there is no real reason to link Higham Hall with the Priory.

When the Crown recovered Higham and Lillechurch manors from Odo of Bayeaux, they were held by Adam, the brother of Eudo Dapifer, the steward of William I, (and subsequently the steward of William II and Henry I). Eudo used the two manors - which would have been a very small part of his land-holding in Kent - to endow Colchester Abbey.[37] When Eudo died in 1120, his considerable estates reverted to the King. Stephen

---

* The grange system was introduced by Cistercian monks and adopted later by other monastic orders. It enabled Abbeys to use self-contained farms staffed by lay brothers to manage more distant land-holdings, although two miles is probably too small a distance for this to be relevant

subsequently granted them as part of a wider grant of Kent land, to reward his loyal chief lieutenant, William of Ypres in 1141. At the time of this grant, the manors of Higham and Lillechurch were still being used to provide income for Colchester Abbey. [38]

Some seven or eight years later years later, William of Ypres, King Stephen and Queen Matilda used Higham and Lillechurch as part of a series of land exchanges to endow their respective religious foundations. Higham priory was one of 170 new religious houses established during Stephen's reign. As well as Higham, for example, Stephen and Matilda founded Faversham Abbey, which they intended as their final resting place[39]. Perhaps the siting of the ferry, and the position of Higham between London and Faversham were factors which contributed to the decision to found a priory in Higham. Whatever the reason, land held by William of Ypres at Faversham was given to Matilda for the Abbey foundation, while William founded Boxley Abbey on land granted land to him. Colchester Abbey received further land in Essex, and the manors of Higham and Lillechurch were released by William for the Queen to use for the endowment of the new priory in Higham.

We should note here that Higham Priory has been inter-changeably named as Higham and Lillechurch priory for most of its history. It was established as a Benedictine nunnery and was intended for the benefit of Stephen and Matilda's one surviving daughter, Mary (born c.1136). She had already been entered into a nunnery in Stratford and was domiciled both there and in Higham with nuns brought from Saint Sulpice in Brittany. [40] Once she moved to Higham, Mary was acknowledged as the Prioress.

After four or five years - sometime between 1155 and 1156 - Mary left Higham for the larger and more prestigious abbey of Romsey. She died in 1182, after a brief period outside the cloister during which she married the then Count of Boulogne, at the behest of Henry II. After Mary's departure, Higham priory declined in national importance. By the late twelfth century, the French influence over the priory had fallen away and the emphasis was on the priory as the centre of the local community, drawing its prioresses from local Kent families such as the Cobhams and Botelers. [41] Three royal writs issued on 12 February 1285 suggested that Edward I stayed at or at least visited the priory perhaps before or after crossing the Thames by the ferry. [42] But there was no other Royal involvement until the sixteenth-century dissolution.

Founding the priory near to the ferry gave it a source of income from those making use of the crossing. It was also adjacent to the existing Saxon/Norman church. Frequent references in the priory accounts to the repair of buildings suggest that the priory had the traditional form of a cluster of associated buildings, and certainly all the archaeological remains have been found in the Abbey Farm area, close to the Church of St Mary (with the exception of a smaller and older chapel by Lillechurch Farm) . There is thus no physical reason, given the distance (one and a half miles) to link Higham Hall with the priory.

Were they then linked by land ownership or use? Considerable archive material relating to the priory is held by St Johns College Cambridge. [43] There are references in the accounts to guests and hospitality and it is to be assumed that the guest housing was within reach of the priory, dairy and kitchen.[44] From the twelfth century, priory land appears to have been leased rather than always farmed directly and other land was granted away from the priory at times. For example, Mary granted lands to Robert, her Chaplain, and to Edward, her servant. [45] It might thus be argued that pieces of priory land granted outside the foundation found their way to becoming 'privately' owned land, and subsequently formed part of the Higham Hall estate. But there is no actual evidence for this.

The priory accounts suggest that the practice of alienating land continued after Mary and throughout the subsequent life of the Priory. While some demesne farming continued into mid-fifteenth century, there is also evidence of considerable amounts of land being rented out from 1430. [46] Writing in his 2006 study of the Priory, Fr Andrew Davis argued that by the early fifteenth century, the greater part of the land was held by tenants. [47] He describes how

'...serjeants were employed for the specific purpose of managing the estates, and paid on an annual salary'. He noted that it is possible that these men lived in demesne property, as their names do not appear among the rentals.[48]

In terms of land use, the accounts suggest that arable farming predominated in Lillechurch manor, with stockholding (pigs, sheep and cattle) in Higham. Corn may have been grown on Lillechurch land and carted on to Higham land for threshing.[49] It is conceivable that Higham Hall Barn was used by the priory for threshing and storage, but given that Abbey farm also had a large barn by the sixteenth century at the latest, which would have been located right next to the priory, this does not seem a particularly convincing argument. In addition, a house called 'Higham Grange' in Hermitage Lane, Higham (although much more modern) provides a credible alternative site for this function (if it existed), particularly since there was also a mill in the same area.[50]

In 1521 the priory was dissolved, ostensibly because of its noticeable decline in size and standards of morality (these have been ably described by Andrew Rootes in his *History of Higham, vol II* amongst others). [51] While the dissolution of Higham Priory preceded the much wider initiative set in motion by Thomas Cromwell in the 1530s, it may have served as a useful model. The then Archbishop of Rochester, Sir John Fisher, cited the immorality of the nuns as his motive, but the lands of the priory provided very useful resources for his project to establish a humanist College in Cambridge. This task had fallen to him in his role as Executor of the late Lady Margaret Beaufort, his patron. With the agreement of King Henry VIII, who briefly seized Lady Margaret's lands on her death, the College of John the Evangelist, Cambridge was endowed with a whole raft of lands, including land at Ospringe, the two manors of Higham and Lillechurch, and the benefice of St Mary at Higham.

The College Archives thus contain extensive records of the lands and management of both manors, from the 1520s until the present day. There is no mention of Higham Hall as part of the priory lands in those archives and nothing to link ownership by the College with subsequent owners of Higham Hall.

Documents held in the National Archives dating from the latter half of the sixteenth century refer to a parcel of land comprising the two manors and the parsonage and rectory of Higham. [52] There is nothing to link either the Rectory or the Parsonage with the Higham Hall site either and the Parsonage was leased for a period by the Boteler family (who are commemorated in St Mary's Church with the tomb of Lady Elizabeth Boteler, who died in 1615). The Manors themselves were let by the College to prominent Kent landowners, such as Sir Peter Manwood and Charles Hales - neither of whom has any subsequent links to Higham Hall. [53]

The Cobham/Brooke Family

So if the Higham Hall estate did not originate from Priory lands, is there an argument that it originally belonged to the other major local landowner - the Cobham/Brooke family? Indeed, did it originally attach to the manor of Higham at all or to another neighbouring manor?

Identifying the boundaries of the estate and of other local land holdings is difficult. It might be a fair assumption for those who know the area that the manor of Higham abutted that of Merston (and subsequently Shorne) but it is not obvious where that boundary was. This becomes even more complicated when 'minor' manors - such as Beckley - are considered. Although Beckley is mentioned as a manor in Domesday, unlike Higham and Shorne, it has not survived as a place into the present day. A F Allen (who has written extensively on the history of Shorne [54]) places Beckley or Bickley around the area of the old British Uralite estate in Higham, stretching north to the marshes bordering the Thames and potentially southwards to at least Lower Chalk Road (see the map on page 44 below). Merston (in all probability) included the Green Farm area, now between Higham and Shorne/Chalk, and the manor of East Chalk is likely to have included the East Court Farm and Filborough Farm areas.

Taken together (which is how they often appear in

pre-seventeenth-century deeds and indentures) Merston, Beckley and East Chalk thus form a distinct wedge between Higham and Chalk, although the shape and extent of that wedge is very difficult to discern. As the seventeenth century progressed, this wedge gradually became subsumed into Higham (Merston and Beckley) and Shorne (Merston and East Chalk) and the lost manors became mere house or cottage names. Allen highlights the fluidity of these boundaries, noting that before the redrawing of parish boundaries in the nineteenth century, the marshland areas of both Shorne and Lower Higham were known as 'Chalk Extra' in various administrative documents.[55]

Is it then the case that the Higham Hall estate, being on the periphery of the Merston/Beckley manors, at some point became detached from it's fellows and became Higham facing, rather than Shorne and Chalk facing with the rest of the Cobham lands? The evidence for this is not as clear as one would like. But it is possible to draw out a plausible chain of ownership which links certain historic owners of the manors of Merston and Beckley with known owners of the Higham Hall estate from around 1630. And whilst incomplete, it is probably the best set of assumptions available to us.

The Merston/Chalk/Beckley area appears as a part of those lands held by Adam from Odo, and then from the King, in the Domesday book. None of these manors are mentioned in the foundation of Higham priory and they appear to become separated from their Higham neighbours when Higham and Lillechurch were bestowed on Colchester Abbey. William Farrar's analysis of the lands of Eudo the Steward suggests some lands in Higham may have been alienated to the de

Cobham family by advantageous marriages.[56] Certainly, the next mention of any of this clutch of land west of Higham is in 1287, when the manor of Randall (in northern Shorne and probably bordering the southern boundary of Merston) is inherited by Henry Cobham, from his father John de Cobham. Beckley is referred to in thirteenth-century knights fee records as belonging to Henry de Cobham.[57]

As they rose to prominence, the de Cobham/Brooke family of Randall extended their estates to include the lands on which they built Cobham Hall and Cooling Castle. The family were thus major landowners in the Hoo, Shorne, Chalk and Gravesend areas by the thirteenth and fourteenth centuries, as well as later holding lands in other parts of Kent of England and Ireland.

In 1540, Sir Thomas Wyatt, who had married into the family, sold a considerable portion of Cobham land in Kent to the King - including unnamed pieces of land in Shorne, Higham and Chalk, and the manors of Rundall (Randall) and Timberwood in Shorne. This was subsequently reunited with the estate when Sir George Brooke bought the land back from the King in 1549 to recreate a coherent landholding in the Shorne and Merston areas. From the 1520s through to the 1550s, the MP for Rochester, Edmund Page held Shorne and Beckley manors together from Sir Thomas Wyatt and subsequently, from Sir George Brooke. Edmund Page's will (1551) refers to the farm of the manor of Beckley and its stock of sheep and cattle, but it is not clear what land this refers to but it may have been Lowells Farm (which was probably in the Chequers area of Higham).

Famously, Sir George's grandson Henry, the eleventh Baron

Cobham, was embroiled in the so called 'Main Plot' against James I in 1603. As a result of this, all of the Cobham lands were attainted and Henry imprisoned in the Tower. Some land, including the manors of Cobham, Temple-Strowde (Strood), Beakley (sic), Randol (Randall) and Gravesend, was placed in trust for Henry's wife, Lady Kildare, to support her during her life. The trustees of the land included Sir John Leveson and Sir Thomas Fane (or Vane), both local MPs and friends of the Cobham family.

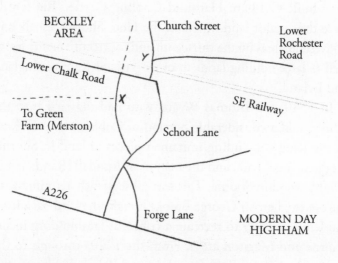

Fig. 2 which shows Beckley Manor in relation to Higham today. X = Higham Hall, and Y= a potential site for Lowells Farm (see below)

Indentures in the Darnley collections in Medway Local Studies and Archives Centre show that some of the seized lands were sold in 1607 to Sir John Dackcombe (then Secretary to Robert Cecil, Earl of Salisbury; Cecil was related to the Cobham family by marriage).[58] These included the manor of Beckley and Lowells Farm in Higham. However, the need to provide for Lady Kildare meant that Dackcombe was only able to buy the reversion of the land, and both Dackcombe and his daughter Dorothy (to whom he willed his interest), died in 1618, while Lady Kildare was still alive and thus in possession of her life interest. It was not until 1628 that Lady Kildare died and, at this point, with no heir to inherit, and significant debts attached to the Dackcombe estate, it seems likely that parcels of the land became available for sale. The effect of the Dackcombe purchase was that Beckley and Lowells may have *de facto* been considered to be a separate parcel.

Looking at the physical evidence, there is a track from Green Farm in Shorne to Higham Hall (see the hand drawn map on the previous page). Seen from this track, the house rises out of the fields and demonstrates little connection with the village of Higham behind it. Instead it looks more like the central farmstead of a distinct area made up of the western part of Higham and the eastern part of Shorne. William Mudge's 1801 map suggests that area was called Beckley. Although the map was drawn centuries later, it has the advantage of recording the landscape before the canal and the railway made the crossroads by the station the dominant feature. Thus Mudge's map shows the Taylors Lane/Chalk Road junction as half of a crossroads which continues through Buckland Farm and links up with Stonewick Bridge and Beckley Hill (now the site of the Uralite factory).

For me, both the physical and the documentary evidence suggest that a more credible account of the origins of the

Higham Hall Estate was that the land was originally part of the lands held by the Cobham family. This land became detached from the larger estate as a result of the sale to Sir John Dackcombe. After the death of the owner, his heir, and of Lady Kildare, it came onto the market in 1628 unencumbered by any other interest in it. It thus formed an attractive parcel of land for the sort of merchant investor from London described by Ann Brown and Lambarde (see page 27 above). And this is also the date from which evidence enables me to put some substantial people in Higham Hall, continuously to until the present day.

Chapter 3

'New Plants' - Samuel Cordwell and his father in law, Richard Machen

The first named person who can be linked to Higham Hall with any degree of certainty is Samuel Cordwell, born in 1596. Cordwell's links with Higham can be traced from the Church of St Mary, where two of the more elaborate memorials commemorate his family. The first is a large table top tomb in the South wall of the Church inscribed:

Here resteth the Body of Mrs Ann Cordewell
Sometime wife to Samuell Cordewell
And daughter of Richard Machen Esq
Who departed this life on the first day of June Anno
Domini 1642
And in ye 28th yeare of her age
She left issue one sonne and two daughters
Luke, Ann and Mary
'God Graunte that thou who yet doth draw thy breath
May'st doe as she did often thinck on death
They that do soe shall doubtlesse meet with blisse
Think still on death thou ne'r wilt doe amisse

The second is a wall mounted memorial above Ann Cordwell's

tomb, which commemorates her grandson, born around the time of the Restoration. This is Samuel Levinge, and documentary evidence exists for his ownership of Higham Hall in the eighteenth century. [59] The memorial records that the grandson of Samuel Cordwell, 'late of this parish [of Higham]', is buried in the same place. (We will see later that the estate appears to have descended to Samuel Levinge via Samuel Cordwell's daughter, Mary).

We can be confident that both Samuel Cordwell and Samuel Levinge owned and occupied the same estate. A small number of field names repeatedly associated with the Higham Hall estate and physically close to the house itself show up in documents dealing with land owned by both the Cordwell and Levinge families and subsequently in title deeds for Higham Hall from the nineteenth century. This makes it highly likely that the land forming the estate was, first, a coherent whole from the seventeenth to the nineteenth centuries and secondly, that references to lands owned by Samuel Cordwell in Higham refer to Higham Hall.

It is worth noting that both Samuel Levinge's memorial and Ann Cordwell's tomb are built into an existing medieval tomb (that of Abbess Joan de Hadloc, of Higham priory, who died in 1348). If nothing else, this would suggest that the Cordwell family were reasonably important in the village- or perhaps they were just good at insisting on a particular burial place that took their fancy!

Samuel Cordwell

There are records for the baptism of a Samuel Cordwell at St Katherine's by the Tower in London, on 7 December 1596- this

Samuel is of the right age for our purposes, with a father named Edmund, and a brother, Robert - names which are confirmed in other source material as pointing to 'our' Samuel Cordwell. [60] Samuel's father, Edmund Cordwell appears to have been a cloth merchant living in Blackfriars and trading in wool and felt in the 1610s. The evidence for this is a writ against him for an unpaid bill - the £45 sought would be considerably greater in today's money (around £4000) and suggest that Edmund Cordwell was a merchant on some scale. [61] Edmund had two sons, Robert and Samuel and two daughters, Elizabeth and Phoebe. When he died in 1622, he left an estate of seven houses in London and Surrey to be divided between his sons. There is, however, no evident link between Edmund Cordwell and Higham.

After his baptism record, Samuel Cordwell next appears when subscribing at Oxford University on 16 April 1613, when he would have been seventeen.[62] At that time matriculation could take place at any point between the ages of thirteen and seventeen, and Samuel's 'subscription' appears to be the process of entering himself for the matriculation exam. He appears again in parish records of St Andrew's Holborn, in London, married to Ellen or Ellinor, and the father of two girls - Ann who was born in April 1625 and died the following month and Susanna, who was born in March 1626 and died in July 1628. At this time, research done by GE Aylmer has identified that Samuel Cordwell was a member of the household of Sir Henry Vane, a courtier in the service of Charles I.[63] Vane rose to be comptroller of the King's household and a prominent statesman, and as such had considerable access to patronage which appears to have benefited Samuel Cordwell in the 1630s.

Certificates of residence for taxation purposes show that Samuel Cordwell was principally resident in London, and in the Royal Household in both 1628 and 1629.[64]

Although there is no firm evidence of this, Samuel's first wife, Ellen appears to have died sometime between 1626 and 1633. [65] She does not appear in any subsequent records and in 1633, when Samuel married his second wife, Ann Machen, in the licence, he is described as 'widower'.

It is through this second marriage that Samuel's first link to Higham appears. Samuel and the eighteen-year-old Ann Machen were married on 26 February 1633 at St Mary Somerset in London, one of the many London churches subsequently destroyed in the Great Fire. His new wife came from Higham and a document from 1664 states that Samuel Cordwell purchased his Higham estate from Richard Machen, Ann's father. [66]

There are two possible routes for the association between Samuel and Richard, some twenty years his senior. The first is through Samuel Cordwell's patron, Sir Henry Vane. The second possible route goes back to Edmund Cordwell, who died in 1622: it is at least possible that Samuel met Ann through previous contacts between Ann's father and his own. Like Edmund, Richard Machen was a cloth merchant and it is not beyond possibility that the two families knew each other from their links in the merchant community in London.

However Samuel and Ann met, the background to Richard and Ann Machen requires a short diversion to Gloucestershire, and to one of the most interesting tombs still visible in Gloucester Cathedral.

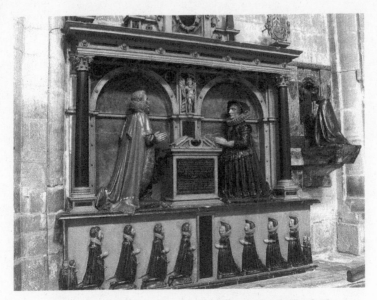

Fig 3 : The Machen tomb in Gloucester Cathedral

The tomb is that of Thomas Machen, mercer and three times Mayor of the City of Gloucester and shows his wife Christian Baston and their thirteen children - seven sons and six daughters. Thomas died in 1614 and in his will, written in 1612, Richard is referred to as Richard Machen of Higham, suggesting that at some point Richard had moved to London, probably to develop his own career, and bought property in Kent with the profits he made. As a younger son, he would have known that the bulk of his father's Gloucester estates would not come his way. In this he was correct, although he did inherit £1500 and a half share of some portions of his father's land. The bulk of the estate went to his mother for her life and then to the family of Henry, Richard's older brother.[67] It was Christian

Baston who laid out the necessary £100 for the elaborate tomb where she was buried with her husband.

Richard Machen married Margaret Davenport - described as the daughter of John Davenport of Davenport, Chester- but we have nothing to link Margaret originally with Higham and she appears in no further records. When Richard is described as *'of Higham'* in his father's will, he would have been approaching 40 and Thomas's will does not suggest that Richard had any children at the time. His mother's will on the other hand, written in 1615, refers to *'my son Richard Machen's daughter'*, which fits with the timing of Ann's Machen (Cordwell)'s birth in 1614. [68] It also suggests that she was Richard and Margaret Machen's first or oldest surviving child, as no other child is mentioned in the will.

It seems to have remained that way. Five years later, the Machens appear to have been living in Higham, as a family: the *'Registrum Roffensis'* refers to a brass plaque formerly in the North Aisle of St Mary's church, commemorating the death of *'three children of R Machen Esq, two sons and one daughter, who severally died in the tract of three years, 1619'*. [69] Ultimately, therefore, there seem to have been four Machen children, of whom only Ann survived.

We can conclude that Richard and Margaret Machen settled in Higham for some years, either renting or owning land there. Richard also bought the Combe estate in St Mary Stoke in the Hoo peninsula as part of his investments in Kent. [70] Richard may still have been trading in cloth in London, using the profits from his business ventures to become one of Lambarde's 'new plants' (page 27 above). Like others of his time and since, he may have wanted to escape the pressures of London life and more pertinently in the sixteenth and seventeenth centuries, the recurrent danger of plague. As well as being close to London, in the seventeenth century Kent was one of the more prosperous places in Britain. Its varied agriculture, including the market gardening introduced by Flemish refugees, made it a significant supplier to London. In addition, Kentish ironwork and shipbuilding and the supply of cloth were second only to the industries of the West Country. [71]

Subsequent documents (see pages 75 and 77, for example) form a chain which link Richard with the Higham Hall estate - and the supposition that this was his home is supported by the lack of any other house or trace of a house in the immediate area suitable for a reasonably wealthy merchant to live in. Other large Higham houses are either later builds (for example, Brick House and Dairy House Farms) or accounted for in Hasted as having other owners (The Hermitage and Great Oakley Farm). [72] The fact that the estate did not become available for sale until around 1628, suggests that the Machens may first have rented it. This would be the logical use of land set aside to provide an income for life, as required by Lady Kildare. On her death, it again seems logical that the current occupier would be well placed to buy it - and this has indeed happened on later occasions in the house's history.

Whatever the precise timing, it appears that Richard Machen purchased the land from the trustees of Lady Kildare. Samuel Cordwell subsequently bought the land from him as part of Ann's marriage settlement, to provide a home for her life. This may have been the arrangement agreed between two families known to each other by a shared background in the cloth trade, as suggested above.

Alternatively, Samuel may have heard of the land for sale and met Ann in the process of the purchase. This seems a little less likely - a case of buying a house and gaining a wife by chance - but it is not impossible. Sir Henry Vane, Samuel's patron, was himself a considerable landowner in Kent, albeit in the Tonbridge area, and related to Sir Thomas Fane (Warden of the Cinque Ports and MP for Dover) one of the original trustees of Lady Kildare's life interest. [73] It may be that family knowledge of the sale was passed on by Vane to Samuel Cordwell. Either way, it is noteworthy that Samuel's purchase was later referred to as being 'held of the King', which may refer back to the original attainder of the Cobham lands in 1603.[74]

The exact circumstances of the purchase, or of how Samuel and Ann came to meet and marry, cannot be proved. But it does seem clear that putting together the evidence of occupation of some land in Higham (consistent with named areas and fields that later formed part of the estate), and the family link from the Cordwell family to the first clearly documented owner (Samuel Levinge), we can place Samuel Cordwell at Higham Hall in the mid to late 1630s, up until his wife Ann's death in 1642. And it is reasonable to suggest that her parents, Richard and Margaret Machen, may have occupied the same house for the preceding fifteen or twenty years.

It is worth pausing at this point to note that the period 1520-1660 was one of growing wealth in the South East. Town life was developing - the population of Gravesend, for example, doubled from 1,000 to 2,000 during the seventeenth century.[75] As has been discussed in Chapter 1, agricultural and transport improvements supported the transformation of the South East into a supplier for national and international markets. The

South East largely avoided the devastation of the Civil War, although changing governments had personal consequences for its wealthier inhabitants.

As a result of this expansion and prosperity, the sixteenth and seventeenth centuries were periods of extensive house building, and of an increase in domestic comfort. [76] In terms of design, houses moved from having a central hearth on the floor of the hall to a central chimney stack between two chambers with the insertion of a front door into a central lobby and a staircase behind the stack. [77] Wash-houses were also beginning to be introduced, particularly by the new rural homeowners moving out from London seeking greater amenity in their country homes. In some cases, houses may have had an additional ground floor room used as a parlour - a combined best bedroom and sitting room. From the mid seventeenth century, the parlour would have a table and chairs added and the beds would move upstairs for greater privacy. This design is evident in the central and oldest part of Higham Hall.

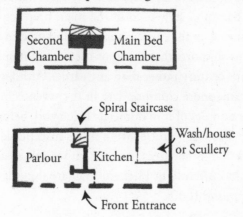

Fig 4: the central and oldest section of Higham Hall

During the first half of the seventeenth century, brick was increasingly replacing timber as the principal method of construction. The typical home was built one room deep, with a gabled roof and dormer windows, which provided usable attics - as in the central block of Higham Hall. Similarly, a typical seventeenth-century fireplace would have a large, wide inglenook, with iron firedogs (known as andirons) supporting the grate and a cast iron fire back protecting the brickwork of the chimney wall. Beams for the inglenook were typically plain, with a chamfered edge, replacing the decorated beams used in Tudor homes. All of these features are or were present in Higham Hall.

Later in the sixteenth century, staircases became more of a feature in a house of any size, with an entrance hall to match. The lack of a grand staircase in Higham Hall also suggests that the house dates originally from the early sixteenth century.

The brickwork in both the house and the garden walls has undergone numerous repairs, and is therefore hard to date, but the most common style used in the main fireplace is Flemish Bond (rather than the earlier, English Bond used in the garden walls). This supports the dating of the central fireplace to the seventeenth century rather than any earlier. Although Flemish Bond became more common late in the seventeenth century, there are examples of it in domestic brickwork before then. As the South Eastern counties were more susceptible to Dutch influences than other areas, it is not impossible that the inglenook bricks currently in Higham Hall are the original bricks dating from the 1630s.

*Fig 5: the inglenook fireplace at Higham Hall with Armada
fireback and brass andirons*

Whilst the fireback in figure 5 above (photograph taken
at Higham Hall while we lived there) may not be an original
Armada fireback - many are actually Victorian copies - the style
is consistent with a Jacobean fireback cast in the Sussex Weald.
The initials IFC stand for 'In Factiem Concepta', meaning in
commemoration of the dead. Although many firebacks of the
time have two side panels, rather than just the central panel
present here, there are other examples of this narrower form. [78]

Thus, with the fireback in its original position and the
andirons in place, the inglenook in Higham Hall gave a very
accurate idea of what a typical seventeenth-century hearth
would look like, with the large chimney stack generating
warmth throughout the centre of the house.

Taken together the documented evidence of Richard
Machen's purchase (which we have placed in 1628), and the
style of and materials in use at Higham Hall, we can fairly

confidently date the house to being an early seventeenth-century construction. It may have been built by Richard Machen in the 1620s, perhaps to replace an earlier, sixteenth-century (Tudor) house that he and his wife had rented.

This idea, that there was an earlier house on the site, is strengthened by the dating of the present garden walls as being of sixteenth-century origin, and thus older than the central portion of Higham Hall.[79] The presence of bee boles (see Chapter 2) as original features of the south courtyard wall lead the conclusion that the walled areas at least were part of a substantial and productive kitchen garden area, rather than a farmyard. Bee boles are wall recesses made to shelter wicker bee hives (or skeps). Used in the Mediterranean since Roman times, other Kentish bee boles dating from the Tudor period have been found in the garden walls of substantial properties - such as the Gatehouse at Eltham Palace, and at Scadbury Manor in St Mary Cray. They are, however, rarely found in farmsteads. [80]

If Richard and Margaret Machen did build Higham Hall in the late 1620s, they did not appear to live there for very long. When Ann Machen married Samuel Cordwell in 1633, Richard had left Higham and Kent, for Wallingford, Berkshire. Their marriage licence reads :

> '[the] marriage between Samuel Cordwell of St Martin in the Fields Widower, 35 and Anne Machen spinster 18, daughter of Richard Machen of Wallingford, Berkshire, gent, who consents, alleged by Robert Cordwell of St Anne's Blackfriars, gent.' [81]

We have no information to tell us when or why Richard

moved. And, after this, he appears no more in the historical record, apart from in a mildly interesting legal case some seven years later. [82]

There is no clear evidence that Samuel Cordwell himself spent much time in Higham after buying the house. But I believe that for a period at least, he saw it as his family home. In addition, his son Luke and daughter in law Eleanor lived there for some of their married life - some of their children were baptised in St Mary's Church. At the very least, it is clear that at the time of Ann Cordwell's death, Higham was considered to be the place she should be buried in. And as I suggest in the next chapter, Higham Hall, and the family life he enjoyed there, seem to have been closer to Samuel Cordwell's heart than his homes in London.

Chapter 4

Samuel Cordwell - gunpowder maker to the King

Henry Vane the Elder (1589-1655) was a prominent politician and statesman. Educated at Brasenose College, Oxford, and Grays Inn, he was knighted by James I in 1611. Having paid £5000 for a position at Court at the age of 23, Vane worked his way up via several diplomatic missions and was made a member of the Privy Council in 1630 and a Commissioner of the Admiralty in 1636. By 1639, he had been appointed Treasurer of the Household by Charles I. Vane's family originated in Hadlow, but established their estate in Shipbourne in Kent.

Sir Henry Vane was a significant figure in Samuel Cordwell's life and his patron. There is no evidence as to how Vane became Samuel's patron - Samuel may simply have been an aspiring and useful member of his household whom Vane wished to reward.[*] But, as his patron, Vane was instrumental in establishing Samuel Cordwell's day job: for some years Cordwell experienced the mixed blessing of being the Gunpowder Manufacturer to King Charles I.

---

[*] In 'The King's Servants', Aylmer describes how offices in the King's household were esteemed as stepping stones to other offices and grants and to royal favours to them, their families and friends.

From the sixteenth century onwards, as Henry VIII began to make inroads into the wealth built up by his father, the Royal Treasury had been under considerable pressure. As a result, many royal privileges and monopolies had been sold to provide income for the Crown. Those relating to the production of armaments were also of significant political interest because of their link to national security. Gunpowder is a mixture of carbon (charcoal), sulphur (brimstone) and potassium nitrate (saltpetre). Since the time of Elizabeth I, the right to produce gunpowder and licences to dig for saltpetre had belonged to the Evelyn family of Godstone in Surrey. [83] The saltpetre was distilled from bird and other excrement, dug out of the ground under dovecotes, barns and private dwellings, and the saltpetre men had extensive and widely resented powers to break into buildings and dig up floors, even those of private houses and farm buildings.[84]

Without going into the detail of the administrative history of the early seventeenth century, the saltpetre licence was one of those that the judiciary focussed on when they tried to loosen the hold of royal officials over private monopolies.[85] The practical effect, in 1625, was that the law was amended to enable saltpetre to be supplied from unlicensed sources - not just those approved or employed by the Royal Ordnance Commissioners. One major result of this was the expansion of imports of cheaper saltpetre from India, brought in by the East India Company.

The East India Company was a major user of gunpowder, principally to supply its own ships and defend its trading posts. So when the Evelyns' patent expired, the Company took over their mills at Chilworth, and set up in production on their own account. [86] The Company's gunpowder production was managed by a man called Edward Collins and, subsequently, by his brother, George, using their imported Indian saltpetre.[87] However, the Company struggled to make a profit on this part of their business and they were probably not wholly disappointed to be warned in December 1634 that the King intended to reinstate the royal monopoly on the manufacture and supply of powder. This would either provide the Company with a guaranteed market if they bought the supplier rights, or alternatively, require them to sell off their mills to the new monopoly owner. Preferring the latter option, production at Chilworth was gradually wound down.

Like Elizabeth before him, Charles I was motivated by two interests in re-establishing control: first, a desire to protect the supply of gunpowder to his own ships and the army; and secondly, to reinstate the valuable monopoly which would supply independent income for the Crown. This was a period of rising prices and as Charles' increasing need for money coincided with his desire to govern without summoning Parliament to agree new taxes, monopolies such as this became all the more important.[88] Given that the Crown bought powder at seven to eight pence per pound and then sold on any surplus powder at one shilling and sixpence per pound, it can be seen how valuable the gunpowder monopoly could be as income.

In April 1635, the minutes of the Court of the East India Company record that 'a gentleman who wishes to remain anonymous' was making enquiries about whether the Company would be willing to sell or lease their mills at Chilworth. [89] Discussions advanced and by July, the Company was negotiating with the King (via Sir Henry Vane) to get the mills running again on a trial basis and to sell him their stocks of saltpetre. In October, the Company agreed to sell 'a goodly proportion [of saltpetre] yearly out of India, for which he would pay ready money'.[90]

As negotiations progressed, it became clear that neither the Evelyn family nor the East India Company wanted to enter into a new contract to supply the King on his terms of seven and a half pence per pound. The Evelyn family had originally been selling at eight and a half pence per pound. So the King and his agent, Sir Henry Vane needed to find a new powder maker - a role which seems to have fallen to Samuel Cordwell, in conjunction with George Collins of Chilworth, who could supply the technical knowledge required. A loan of £2000 was agreed from the Crown, to enable Chilworth Mills to be expanded and, in February 1637, Samuel leased the mills and bought the equipment from Edward Collins' widow, Sarah.

Keith Fairclough has made a study of gunpowder supply during the 1630s and 1640s. He has suggested that whilst Samuel Cordwell had no history of powder making, he was the dominant partner in this contractual relationship, as a result of his connection to Vane, and possibly by virtue of his existing financial resources.[91] Whilst George Collins was previously linked with the Chilworth mills and lived and worked there throughout this period, Samuel appears to have lived and worked mostly in London. Documents record an order that saltpetre supplies be delivered to his warehouse in Southwark, for example. Throughout the existing records, it is Cordwell who is referred to as the King's powder maker and it is he who deals with the King, the powder supply committee and the House of Commons over the orders and bills for his product.

Samuel Cordwell's monopoly was granted by an Act of Parliament of September 1636, which stated

> ' whereas we have been pleased to assume and take into our hands , and for our own use and benefit, all the Salt-Petre which shall be made within our Kingdom and dominion of Wales or imported into the same from foreign parts, and to sell and distribute all such powder as is or shall be made thereof, to such our subjects, as for their use and provision shall desire the same, over and above that which shall be necessary for our own service; and are minded that the making of SaltPetre and Gunpowder, and the sale of Gunpowder, shall hereafter [be] managed by one and the same person for our benefit.
>
> And whereas a contract was lately made on our behalf with Samuel Cordwell and George Collins, gentlemen, for the sole working and converting into Gunpowder of all SaltPetre, as well got, digged, and made within this realm of England [or imported] ...they are for the space of 13 years... to bring and deliver unto our stores within our Tower of London...' [92]

The contract was signed and dated 24 December 1636, at Westminster; Cordwell's patron, Sir Henry Vane, was one of the witnesses. (Incidentally, a deed in the papers of Sir Bulstrode Whitlocke (a prominent Civil War era lawyer) suggests that at some point in the 1620s or 1630s, Samuel Cordwell lent Sir Henry Vane a sum of money to assist with the purchase of Raby Castle in Northumberland.[93] As usual, patronage was eased by the exchange of hard cash!)

Despite his lack of experience, Samuel appears to have made

a success of his new venture, at least to begin with, and in February 1639, the King granted Samuel (but not George Collins) a gift of £150 pounds, in gratitude for his work in the supply of gunpowder. [94]

As an additional reward, on 2nd July 1640, Samuel was granted the reversion to the position of 'official custodian of Lions and Leopards for life' (although there is no evidence that he ever succeeded to this post). The honorific (and lucrative) position of Keeper of the Royal Menagerie at the Tower of London - the formal title of this office - had frequently been linked to offices supplying armaments, which were stored at the Tower.[95]

The menagerie was a popular tourist attraction at the time, and were he to have succeeded to it, the income would have been a very useful addition. In practice, all Samuel gained was the ability to hand the reversion on to his son, but again, there is no evidence that his son got any benefit from it either. A reversion - which only conveyed a future interest in an office - was often of limited use because of the number of people ahead of you in the queue. This certainly seems to have applied to the Cordwells.

The evidence suggests that whilst Samuel lived mainly in London and travelled to Chilworth when he needed to, his country property was in Higham. In his work on 'The Civil Service of Charles I', GE Aylmer writes that as early as the 1630s, a number of officials had country properties at which they would spend time during the summer, while 'entrusting it to a capable steward or bailiff' at other times. [96] Some Londoners might also let their country estate to a tenant farmer and it is possible that, as Samuel's business interests became more time consuming, he did this too. Later records place him and his family in Lambeth Marsh rather than in Kent. However, at least during the 1630s, his identification as 'Samuel Cordwell of Higham' and the links that Ann and his children had subsequently with Higham suggest that a good deal of time was spent there by the family.

Samuel supplied powder to the King from 1636 until his death in 1648. During the earlier part of this period, he and Ann had three children - Luke born in 1636, the year of his father's great change in fortune, and two daughters, Ann, and Mary. Luke (also referred to at various points in his life as Luke Cordwell of Higham) was baptised in St Mary of Lambeth church late in 1637 and Mary was baptised in Lambeth on 31 July 1640. A fourth child, Martha, was baptised in Lambeth in January 1642, although she then disappears from the records, suggesting that she died shortly after her birth. Samuel's wife Ann died on 1 June that same year, aged just 28, leaving Samuel a widower for the second time. While it is possible that Ann and Martha died from the same illness, the child is neither buried with her mother, nor mentioned on her tombstone, so it seems more likely she died in London, shortly after her birth and baptism.

On her death, as we have seen, Ann was buried in a prominent tomb in St Mary's Church in Higham, leaving Samuel alone with three children aged under seven.

The course of Samuel's powder monopoly did not run entirely smoothly, despite his early successes. From October 1637, Cordwell and Collins were granted the right to 'repair decayed gunpowder', to entrench their monopoly, and in 1642, Cordwell received the right to supply the Navy directly.

[97] But the business seems to have required a great deal of day to day management. Although Samuel more than doubled the output of Chilworth from fifty to 120 barrels per week, there were numerous difficulties relating to the supply of materials and payment. In 1637, Samuel petitioned the King about the shortage of saltpetre available to him - if this was not increased 'my mills must stand still'. In 1640, he complained that he was owed £4,000 by the Crown.[98] In March 1641, Samuel petitioned the King to ensure that any applications from competitors to make powder be referred to the Privy Council, as he was afraid that the high stock levels he had put aside to hold to meet orders would ruin him if cheaper supplies came onto the market. [99] When in July that year, a bill was introduced to end the gunpowder monopoly, Samuel had to start supplying private customers to protect his income.

It is probably the case that Samuel's investment was only saved by the hugely increased demand for gunpowder resulting from the Civil War. During the war, Parliamentary forces controlled the County of Surrey and so the location of the mill dictated that Samuel supplied them with powder. From 1642, he began negotiating with Parliament directly. As Keith Fairclough succinctly puts it

'The absence of personal records... means that his attitudes to this conflict cannot be assessed; he may have had conflicting loyalties. He had emerged [close to] the Royal Household and had entered the gunpowder industry as a supporter of the King's policy, but he was to become a major supplier of gunpowder to Parliament during the Civil war. Given the location of Chilworth mills, he was obliged to

do so or face complete financial ruin, but he had suffered financially from the King's inability to meet his bills.[100]

The South East region was broadly sympathetic to the Parliamentary cause and as Brandon points out, the main effect of the Civil War here was to increase the role of middling gentry in economic and political affairs. [101] Men like Samuel Cordwell were in a good position to take advantage of this trend.

Although the mills were pulled down on Parliament's orders in November 1642, to prevent them falling into the hands of the advancing Royalists, they were not rendered unrepairable and production for Parliament was up and running again at Chilworth by March 1643. That profits remained precarious, though, is illustrated by the Calendar of the Proceedings of the Committee for the Advancement of Money 1642-56.[102] This committee monitored and enforced the payment of taxes, and the records for 1644 list the *'persons having had notice of the sums assessed and refused to pay or lapsed the days of payment'*. The list includes *'Sam. Cordwell assessed at £100'*. On 25 January 1644, the Committee ordered *'Sam. Cordwell Gunpowder maker, Southwark, …to be brought up in custody to pay his account'*.

On 30th January, Samuel appeared before the committee and was successful in persuading them that his cash flow problems were caused by the Government. The committee thus ordered that *'after he has received £500 of the monies owing to him by the state, he pay in £500 or powder to that value towards his assessment.'* On 3 February he was summoned again, but pleaded that he had received nothing of his payments, and argued that that the forced damage to his mills meant he could not afford to pay. On his third appearance on 18 November 1644, the Committee had obviously lost patience with Samuel's excuses, and ordered that he be sent to prison for failing to pay his assessment. There is no evidence of whether he paid up at that point or served his time. Either way, Samuel Cordwell continued to supply powder to Parliament until his death in 1648. It was perhaps his links with the leaders of the Parliamentary forces that led to the marriage of his son Luke to a wealthy heiress on the Parliamentary side, Eleanor Roberts.

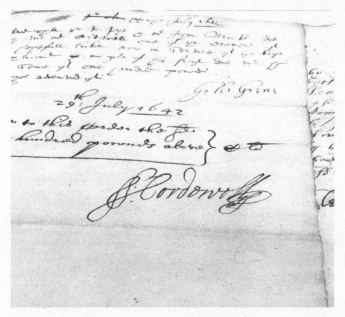

Fig 6: the signature of Samuel Cordwell on a receipt for a payment in respect of his ship, 'The Hopeful Luke'

Following Ann's death, and given the burden of his work, Samuel was wholly based in London after 1642. He is from then more commonly described as living in Lambeth Marsh, a rural area with individual houses clustered around a through road, leading from Westminster into Surrey. His will confirms that Higham Hall was let at this time to a Francis Wakeland, of whom little is known, unfortunately.

In March 1645, Samuel married a third time, in Greenwich, to Sarah Cropley, herself a widow. Their child, Sarah, (Samuel's sixth daughter but only the third to survive) was baptised in Lambeth in September 1646.

Samuel died in Lambeth, in February 1648 leaving children aged twelve, ten, eight and eighteen months. In his will he refers to himself as '*Samuel Cordwell of Higham*' and stated that he should be buried in Higham, but sadly, it is not clear that this took place. His will shows that he held other land in Kent: the Combe estate on the Hoo peninsula, which he had bought, and land in Surrey, centred in Abinger and Abingworth. As we have said, the estate and farm in Higham are described as being leased out. In his will, Samuel refers directly to an Orchard he planted named 'Winters', 'which has determined the tithe for his alms payments to the poor of Higham for three years'. It is this the name of this orchard which is common to the Higham Hall estate in 1648 and to the catalogues of sale from the Victorian period, which we shall come on to later.

Much of the will covers the finer details of the marriage settlement with Sarah Cropley - which would certainly set her up for life - but it also shows that Samuel had investments in two ships (one named the Hopeful Luke), and that he did not forget the family of George Collins - leaving £100 to his widow, and £20 to apprentice his son John 'in some good way and calling'. Whilst the bulk of his goods and chattels from his London home are left to his wife and youngest child, the bulk of his estate - the land in Higham (and the contents of the house there), and the lands in Combe (in Hoo) and in Surrey - are left to Luke (together with the reversion to the menagerie), and his executors are instructed to

> *'be careful and diligent to get my two daughters Ann and Mary religiously and virtuously brought up and educated'.*[103]

The will shows a distinct split between Samuel's old and new families. Sarah is given the money and investments due to her under her marriage settlement (which include a house not yet purchased) and the responsibility to care for and educate their infant daughter. On the other hand, Luke, Ann and Mary are left to the care of Samuel's executors, his brother Robert and 'my loving friend Nathaniel Sykes, citizen and fishmonger of London', and these two are entrusted with the management of Samuel's landed estates and remaining residual cash, for the benefit of the three children. Rings *'which I had before marriage with my now wife'* are left to Ann and Mary.

The will says that ' *all my goods, household stuff brass, pewter, beddings, linens and furniture whatsoever at my house at Higham aforesaid shall remain there unto my son and be by my executor carefully preserved for him and his wife'*. It is this perhaps of all the evidence that suggests that Samuel had an established and comfortable home in Higham as his family home as well as any London residence he used. Samuel's wish to be buried in Higham, with his second wife, suggests that this was might have been the happiest and most meaningful period of his life.

The will does not deal with the powder contracts or lease

of the mill but it is clear from other documents that these passed to Samuel's brother Robert on his death. In March 1648, the Ordnance instructed that Robert should receive salt-petre in future and he continued to produce gunpowder for a further two years, renewing the lease on the mills in 1649.[104] Unfortunately, Robert himself then died and, whilst his widow, Mary continued running the business for a few months, she sold her share of the business in 1650 to a consortium of entre-preneurs, led by her brother in law, Josias Dewye. [105] From that point on, the history of Higham Hall has no further links to the history of gunpowder.

Chapter 5

Cordwell to Levinge - London lawyers

Luke Cordwell

Robert Cordwell administered Samuel's estate between 1648 and 1650, as Samuel's son Luke was only twelve when his father died. After Robert's own death, administration of the estate fell to Nathaniel Sykes - who is described in the will as a 'loving friend' of Samuel Cordwell, and a London fishmonger.

It is possible, however, that Nathaniel did not make a particularly assiduous executor. At least three legal actions were brought on Luke's behalf in the period 1651 to 1656 by his guardian John Clarke.[106] These concern the recovery of goods and chattels taken from the house at Higham by Mary Cordwell (Robert's widow and thus, Luke's aunt). These goods were passed on to her daughter, Grace Sanders, and John Clarke had to sue Grace and her husband for their recovery.

A fourth action concerned the legacies owed to Luke's sisters, Ann and Mary. Samuel Cordwell was still owed money by the Crown on his death. And this suit suggests that Mary Cordwell sold a stock of gunpowder after her husband's death, but neglected to pass the value on to her nieces, although it would have gone part way to settling the legacies due to them under their father's will. This action was brought by Sir Bulstrode Whitelocke - an eminent lawyer of the period, and Treasury Solicitor - either in his capacity to protect the inheritance of wards (minors) or perhaps because Whitelocke was familiar to the Cordwell family though his previous work for Sir Henry Vane.[107]

Luke matriculated at St John's College, Oxford University in 1653 aged seventeen. College records suggest that he came and went from College over the next three years, finally studying at the Inner Temple in London during 1653 to 1654.[108] He graduated from Oxford in February 1655 but there is no evidence of what he then went on to do, although one might assume he went into the Law. His next appearance in a historical record is his marriage in 1664, at the age of 28. Luke's bride, Eleanor, was the daughter of a prominent and wealthy Parliamentarian - Sir William Roberts of Neasden (1606-1662).

Roberts had made his fortune by a combination of marriage, and buying up confiscated church land. A friend of Oliver Cromwell and Lord of the Manor of Neasden, Roberts conducted marriages at his house and took charge of the registers during the Interregnum. Although he was a member of the Parliament who conferred the title of Lord Protector on Oliver Cromwell, Sir William managed to avoid a riskier assignment, declining the invitation to join the bench of judges who tried and condemned King Charles I to death. Consequently, he regained the favour of the Crown at the Restoration and was knighted by King Charles II, although losing some of his considerable holdings of church land in the process.

Roberts had a large family of fifteen children, of whom Eleanor was one of the youngest (born in 1641). Marrying off this substantial brood was a task in itself, which might explain why the comparatively lowly Luke Cordwell was considered an eligible husband for Eleanor. Their lengthy marriage settlement, however, illustrates that Eleanor's mother, Dame Ellinor Roberts, at least was determined that her daughter's interests would be protected by herself and a trusted son in law (Samuel Gibbs, married to Eleanor's older sister Jane) who would be more experienced in law and business than Luke. [109]

Luke married Eleanor Roberts on 17 November 1664, at St Mary's Willesdon. Parish records from Willesden and Higham suggest that they had four daughters - Eleanor, baptised in Willesdon on 11 September 1665, Anne, baptised in Willesden on 18 March 1667, Mary, baptised in Higham on 29 January 1669, and Jane, baptised in Willesdon on 9 February 1671. Mary died and was buried in Willesden in June 1670, and it is not completely clear from the subsequent history of Higham Hall whether the young Eleanor, Anne, or indeed Jane survived. Luke himself died early in the marriage - in September 1670, before the birth of his daughter Jane and not long after Mary's death. He left Eleanor with daughters of five and three and one yet unborn. He was buried the following day, in St Marys church, Higham, described as 'gent' in the burial register. He was aged just thirty-four.

At both his matriculation at Oxford and on his entry to the Inner Temple, Luke was described as Luke Cordwell of Higham. Various deeds from this period refer to the estate as land belonging to Mr Cordwell, or as Madam Cordwell's land. Clearly the Cordwells' ownership of the land continued and, again, it is tied in to the Higham Hall estate by the reference to known field or orchard names - Hobletts and Winters in this case. For example, an indenture dated 23 January 1685, which refers to land rented by Henry Phipps of Higham '*in Hobletts and Winters and joining Mr Cordwell's*'. [110]

The birth of one child in Higham and Luke's burial there suggest that this set of Cordwells had lived in the village and in Higham Hall at some point. They seem also to have resided in Willesden and it is likely that Eleanor returned to her family home after Luke's death. Later sources suggest that Elinor began leasing out at least some of the Higham land, and possibly the house itself. But the Hearth tax, levied between 1662 and 1689, gives 'Cordwell' as the name of the owner, confirming that she had not sold it. The tax records list twelve hearths for Higham Hall and its associated cottages; all of these would have been internal fireplaces, as working hearths, such as those in brewhouses, were not taxed. [111] Similarly, Mrs Cordwell is the name of one of the Parish Ratepayers for Higham in 1700.

In this period, agriculture remained a profitable venture so it was sensible to lease land out for a secure income, rather than simply sell it and realise the value. In 1649-50 for example, London received 989 shipments of corn, of which 527 came from Kent. [112] The principal crops grown in North Kent were wheat, barley, peas, beans and oats, with sheep kept for meat and for manuring the land. Fruit growing was also popular locally. As Brandon comments

> '*North Kent's rural economy was quite simply the most diverse and prosperous in the South east*' [113]

To picture the land at this time, we are reliant on Celia Fiennes, who describes travelling from Rochester to Gravesend,

'...in sight of the River Thames, which is all by the side of cherry grounds that are of several acres of ground, and runs quite down to the Thames, which is convenient to convey the cherries to London, for here the Great produce of Kent fruites which supplies the Town and Country with the Kentish Cherries, a good sort of Flemish Fruite.' [114]

In July 1682, Eleanor had to fight off a legal challenge for the ownership of the estate. This was brought by Maurice Bockland and Giles Faunton, who appear to have been as unfamiliar to Eleanor as they are to me from my researches into the history of the estate. Nonetheless, they argued that the land had been promised to their forebears by King Charles I. Fortunately for us, Eleanor's defence statement contains the information that the estate was bought by Samuel Cordwell from his father in law, Richard Machen, and the documentary evidence of this was sufficient to convince the Chancery Court of Eleanor's title to the land. [115]

After her death, Eleanor was buried in St Mary's Higham, on 28 January 1709. Then aged sixty-eight, she had survived Luke by thirty-nine years and is described as a widow. Her burial in Higham rather than Willesden suggests an emotional tie to the village and their home there, as well as a wish to be buried with her late husband, despite their short marriage.

Samuel Levinge

The next owner who can be identified is Samuel Levinge - nephew of Luke and Eleanor Cordwell, and the grandson of Samuel Cordwell. So despite the change in family name, Higham Hall remained with descendants of Samuel Cordwell for a further seventy years. As we have seen, the evidence for this can still be seen in the South wall of St Mary's church in Higham.

Following Eleanor Cordwell's death, the land in Higham (at least) appears to have passed to the family of her sister in law Mary Cordwell, born in 1640, Luke's younger sister. Mary married Francis Levinge on 6 January 1658, at the age of eighteen, in the parish of St Bartholomew the Great, London. Their only surviving child Samuel was born eight years later, in 1666. * The fact that he was baptised at St Mary's in Higham, on February 14 1666, is a little puzzling. Earlier I explained that Luke and Eleanor seem to have been quite closely linked to Higham, although they also lived in Willesden at times. In 1666, Luke was still alive and daughters born to him and Eleanor in 1665 and 1667 were baptised in Willesden. Were Luke and Eleanor living with her parents, while Mary and Francis lived in Higham? We cannot tell, but it was plausible that Eleanor would prefer to live with her mother and sisters while she was caring for very small children.

It is possible that one at least of Luke and Eleanor's daughters outlived them. Parish records refer to a Jane Cordwell, who died and was buried in Higham in September 1741. Conceivably, she was their daughter, Jane, born in 1671. If it is her, she would have been aged seventy at her death. Jane was born posthumously and may have thus been omitted from any will that her father had made. It possible that Jane had a life interest

---

* St Mary's Parish Registers record the burial of a Thomas Levine (adult) in August 1695. This may have been an older or younger brother of Samuel Levinge (it is not a common name for Higham) but as he died before Eleanor Cordwell, he does not figure in our history.

in Higham Hall, which is not evident, and that the estate only passed to Samuel Levinge on her death in 1741, some thirty years after the death of Eleanor.

The absence of a will for Luke Cordwell is frustrating but some clues can be gleaned from Eleanor's defence document referred to above (page 77). This refers clearly to the Higham Hall estate being Eleanor's jointure - in other words, a life interest only, available to her until her death, or until she remarried. This implies that the full title to the land was vested elsewhere, and also that Eleanor would not have been able to dispose of it by will herself. Thus, before his death, and having access to more than one estate himself, Luke might have wished to make provision for his sister Mary, and her (perhaps) less well provided for husband. If Mary and Francis brought up Samuel in Higham Hall, the arrangement might have been for him to inherit the estate on Eleanor's death. Any such arrangement might have required or encouraged Mary and Samuel to provide a home for the unmarried Jane, or any other surviving daughters. Or, the estate may simply have passed to the next surviving male heir - his nephew, Samuel Levinge. This would not prevent Samuel from supporting Jane in a not uncommon arrangement - as a bachelor, Samuel may well have welcomed a female cousin to keep house for him.

We cannot tell the precise arrangements or the motivation behind them, but the facts are that Mary's son, Samuel Levinge was baptised in Higham in 1666, and he became the owner of the Higham Hall Estate. Both Samuel Levinge and Jane Cordwell were subsequently buried in Higham. Samuel's burial in November 1748, at the age of eighty two years, was a grander affair than Jane's and his tomb provides the evidence for his heritage. Samuel is described as '*Grandson of Samuel Cordwell, late of this parish*' and his memorial displays the Leving/Levinge family crest of three scallop shells.

Fig 7 : Samuel Levinge's memorial with Ann Cordwell's Tomb beneath, St Mary's Church, Higham

Fig 8 : The Levinge Crest

The Leving/Levinge family originated in Warwickshire. LF Salzman in the '*Victoria County History for the County of Warwick*'(1947 pp19-21) records how the manor of Baddesley Ensor was originally held by the Cokayne family, and sold to Francis Leving at the beginning of the reign of James 1 (in other words, the early 1600s), and Professor Robert Palmer (Cullen Professor of Law, University of Houston) records an Attorney called Francis Levinge practising in Warwickshire in the same period, in his '*Attorneys in Early modern England and Wales*'. [116] This Francis is likely to be the father or an uncle of 'our' Francis, because of the dates, but they share the same scallop shell coat of arms.

The Levinge family produced a number of prominent lawyers, including Timothy Levinge, MP for Derby (1621-1628) and Sir Richard Levinge, Solicitor General of Ireland, (1690-94 and 1704). [117] The Record of Admissions of the Inner Temple refer to Samuel Levinge as the Grandson of Timothy

Levinge, former Master of the Bench of the Inner Temple and refer to his 'special' admission, as if some kind of advantage had been conferred on him by his relative. [118]

It is not surprising then that Samuel Levinge of Higham followed the same profession. He became a barrister of the Inner temple, admitted on 24 November 1689 (aged twenty-three). In the late seventeenth and early eighteenth centuries, this profession was considered to be a good money earner, attracting the younger sons of rural gentry, often enabling them to purchase their own small estates from the profits in later life. As well as drawing up legal documents, attorneys at this point in time were responsible for arranging loans and mortgages, and Samuel certainly took advantage of this part of his brief. In 1705, he is described as a resident of London, but that, of course, does not preclude him from having Higham as a country estate.

There is some evidence that Samuel may have leased out the land (or parts of it) during the early stages of his career - for example, in 1716, an indenture made between Percival Hart and Dorothy Masters (widow) refers to a messuage, garden, stable and barn and '*half an acre in Hobletts and half an acre lying within grounds of Madam Elinor Cordwell*' [ibid], together with '*two acres of Childe's Wood, half an acre in Winters, eight acres in Turks dale and five yards of common land adjacent to Madam Cordwell's.*' *

However, Samuel's will (written on 2 April 1747) supports the belief that he lived at least sometimes in Higham Hall and

---

* Obviously Eleanor was dead by this point, but it is common in older documents for land to be referred to by the names of previous owners - they may be more widely known locally and thus the land more identifiable this way.

probably more often as he became older. In describing Higham Hall he refers to '*all my plate… and everything that is used in my house*', which is an unlikely formulation to have used if the house had been let, unfurnished, to a tenant farmer. The will also refers to '*live and dead stock in and about my farm there…*' [119] The will refers to other property in Chalk, Higham, Cliffe and Frindsbury, as well as land in Sussex and Suffolk, suggesting that Samuel Levinge was of substantial means.

While some of the land may well have come to him from his Cordwell grandfather, it is clear that a proportion of his wealth came to him from advantageous deals which he made in return for the loan of various amounts of money. For example, in 1737, loans of £100 and £500 made to Mary Sheldon (a spinster living in Hanover Square in London), were secured against the manor of Howe Court which she owned in East Sussex. [120] After Samuel's death in 1748, a document was drawn up allowing Samuel's heir to benefit from the redemption of these loans to the tune of £673 for the principal sum and £368 10 shillings for eleven years of interest payments. [121] Mary Sheldon's own heir could not afford to redeem the estate and it was instead sold on by Samuel's heir, Elizabeth, at further profit, for a total of £1470 to Thomas Pelham, heir to the Duke of Newcastle's Sussex estates. [122]

In his will, Samuel left all his land and personal property to his cousin Elizabeth Levinge, save for a few small cash bequests to other cousins. This does reinforce the conclusion that he was both unmarried and died without issue. The inheritance established Elizabeth Levinge as a woman of property and a document was drawn up before Samuel's death to secure his planned legacy to Elizabeth and her first born son on her marriage. Other records date Elizabeth's birth as 1720 and both the pre-nuptial deed and her marriage certificate refer to her as Elizabeth Levinge of Higham. It is thus conceivable that Elizabeth lived with her uncle at Higham Hall, perhaps after the death of Jane Cordwell, but there is no firm evidence to this effect. Nor do we know who her parents were, although it is clear that she came from the Warwickshire Levinge side of Samuel's family, rather than the London or Higham Cordwells. Perhaps therefore, she had been informally 'adopted' by her childless uncle, to provide for her future, in return for a period of keeping his house. Either way, Elizabeth was twenty eight and newly married when she inherited the estate and her uncle's other lands, and she became the means by which Higham Hall passed into the hands of a wealthy Dutch lawyer and art collector.

Chapter 6

The Dutch connection : the Van Heythuysen family

Gerard Levinge van Heythuysen is one of the more surprising owners of Higham Hall. It is worth taking a diversion into his background and looking at the circles he moved in. His holding of the land and the use to which he put it is an illustration of how property can pass in unexpected directions as a result of the vagaries of inheritance and marriage.

The Dutch community in London, both craftsmen and financiers, had originally been established with the encouragement of Edward VI, who was looking to establish a community of Protestant thinkers (and hopefully evangelists for their religion) in his capital. In 1550, London's community of '*Germans and other strangers*' had been granted the use of the church of the Augustinian Friars, in Bishopsgate in the City of London, and the community had coalesced around it, with the church of the Austin friars forming a central part in their religious and social life. Originally a friary church, the building and its surrounds had been confiscated during the Dissolution of the monasteries.

Whilst Edward made no attempts to curtail or oversee the religion preached in the new Protestant Church once it had been made over to them, it was briefly lost to the community during Queen Mary's reign. The church was then granted back on Elizabeth I's accession in 1558. It remains known as 'the Dutch Church' to this day, with some services conducted in Dutch. Pragmatic in religious terms, Queen Elizabeth was primarily interested in the economic benefits of immigrant craftsmen and textile workers and whilst she ensured that the Dutch Church was overseen by the Bishop of London, the community around the church was allowed to grow and become prosperous. It was well established and thriving in London by the mid seventeenth century.[123]

Whilst Dutch immigration was originally provoked by religious persecution, by the late seventeenth century the community was augmented by entrepreneurs attracted by the success of the new community. It is fair to say the Van Heythuysen family might have fallen into either category. Van Heythuysen family research suggests that they came from the small town of Heythuysen in Limburg; a Catholic province of Holland near to the German border.[124]

The first recorded 'English' van Heythuysen is Gerrard, who died in 1691 or 1692; Gerrard was a protestant merchant and he married into a prominent family - the Lodwicks. His new brother-in-law, Francis Lodwick (1619-1694), is described as an important figure in seventeenth-century thought, who associated with Sir Christopher Wren and Robert Hooke (the architect and natural philosopher). Coming thus from a *rich and intellectually curious family… who were pillars of the London Dutch Community*', Gerrard's wife, Anna, brought social cachet to the van Heythuysen family, which helped to establish them in seventeenth-century London society. As business men and lawyers, the van Heythuysen family had London homes in the Holborn area, close to the Inns of Court.

On her death in 1693, Anna van Heythuysen left the bulk of her estate to her husband's nephew, another Gerard van Heythuysen. Since she had a son and daughter of her own, the presumption must be that her husband had sufficient means to provide handsomely for their own offspring on his death. Anna was a wealthy woman: her will left money, gifts and money for mourning clothes to her many relatives.

It was Anna's great-grandson, Delme van Heythuysen, who married into the Levinge family and provided the link to Higham Hall. We can speculate whether Elizabeth Levinge met her future husband through her cousin Samuel's connections in the Temple as by this time, several members of the van Heythuysen family were practising lawyers. Delme himself served as Commissioner for Bankrupts from 1765-1776 (a judicial appointment made by the Lord Chancellor and attached to the Chancery Courts).

As we have seen, Samuel Levinge's Higham, Chalk, Cliffe and Frindsbury estates were inherited by Elizabeth Levinge. A pre-marriage contract drawn up on 6 February 1748, refers to her planned marriage to Delme van Heythuysen (a barrister of the Inner Temple). This contract provided that the Levinge estate would remain her property on her marriage but that, once her eldest son was born, she would hold this land jointly with him.

There is certainly no evidence that Delme and Elizabeth van Heythuysen lived in Higham Hall after their marriage in February 1748 and it seems very unlikely that they did. Although Samuel had clearly lived there, the estate now appears to become simply part of Elizabeth's inheritance, settled on her and her son: an investment rather than a family home. It remained in her sole hands, until the birth of her first son, Gerard Levinge van Heythuysen, in 1751. From then on, the property was jointly owned by Elizabeth and Gerard until its sale in 1781.

While the Machins and Cordwells are examples of middling gentry content with a modest country home, the van Heythuysens appear to have been of a different social standing, wealthier and with the taste and means for larger country houses. This can be assumed in part from the society Elizabeth's son, Gerard, kept. Although the document itself is out of print and impossible to find, there are extant references to him exhibiting a selection of valuable paintings, along with the founder of the National Gallery, as follows:

> ' a capital selection of valuable paintings, part the Property of John Julius Angerstein and Part the Property of Gerard Levinge van Heythuysen, …works of the Italian, French, English, Fleming and German Schools',

This exhibition took place in 1800. John Angerstein, Gerard's fellow exhibitor was a Russian of unclear parentage who came to London in 1749 in the household of a merchant, Andrew Thompson. Thompson worked closely with the Muilmans, another leading family in the Anglo-Dutch community and, as Angerstein's mentor, introduced him to both the Muilmans, and the new insurance industry growing up in the London coffee houses. With his wealth thus built on international trade and maritime insurance, John Angerstein rose to a prominent position in London, joining the committee of Lloyds in 1786, and serving as its chairman in 1795-6. Naturalised in 1770, Angerstein became a British philanthropist, supporting Christ's Hospital School, helping to establish the Royal Institution and leading Lloyds' involvement in the provision of lifeboats for sailors.[125]

Angerstein collected art on a significant scale - two of his most famous purchases were Raphael's 1512 portrait of Pope Julius II and del Piombo's 'Raising of Lazarus', which are currently in the National Gallery. Always keen to let others see his pictures, Angerstein was an early patron of the 'Betterment Society', which encouraged private collectors to exhibit their pictures, for students to copy, and for interested members of the public to view.[126] Two exhibitions took place in London in 1806, featuring a number of old masters owned by Angerstein. It was perhaps not surprising after his death, therefore, that a detailed catalogue of his paintings was produced, and in 1823, the Government bought all of Angerstein's collection, and opened his art collection (and his Pall Mall house) to the public as the National Gallery, in April 1824.[127]

Whether the exhibition with Angerstein was a one-off or a frequent action, Gerard Levinge Van Heythuysen was clearly a collector of art with the means to support his interest. Moreover, the evidence shows his life was centred on London and other van Heythuysen properties rather than in North Kent. Born in 1751, three years after his parents' marriage, Gerard was the only surviving child. He therefore stood to inherit all of his parents' wealth and estates, in Suffolk, on his father's side, and in Kent and in Sussex on his mother's. In July 1772, Gerard entered Lincoln's Inn, and in 1777, he followed (or perhaps succeeded) his father into the office of

Commissioner of Bankrupts.

In October of the previous year, in 1776, Gerard had married Amy Mighells of Lowestoft and the couple went on to have twelve children, eleven of whom survived into adulthood. Their children were variously born in London (Southampton Buildings in Holborn), Cromer in Norfolk, and St Mary Cray in Kent. This supports the conclusion that Gerard and Amy never lived at Higham Hall. Documents show that Gerard bought and sold land near Cromer in 1785 and, in 1795, he purchased and extensively remodelled a thirty bedroomed house near Christchurch, Highcliffe Castle.

The van Heythuysen's main home appears to have been in St Mary Cray, some twenty miles from Higham. We know this from Hasted's description of the village (written between 1778 and 1799) which refers to there being two principal seats in the locality, one of which '... *has been purchased by Gerard Levinge van Heythuysen Esq, who resides in it, the present owner of it.*' Hasted says this purchase took place sometime after 1775 and five of the van Heythuysen children were baptised in the church at St Mary Cray between 1787 and 1794, although the particular house Gerard purchased or had built there cannot be identified.

It is perhaps not surprising that Gerard settled in this area - John Angerstein himself had bought Kent House in Beckenham in 1784, and in the late 1760s, a wealthy Dutch man (Herman Behrens) had built Kevington Hall in St Mary Cray. This suggests south-east London and the fringes of west Kent was considered a desirable area for wealthy London lawyers and entrepreneurs to establish a country home. There is no evidence that Higham was considered in the same light.

It might even have been the case that the Higham Hall estate was sold to release capital for the purchase of the house in St Mary Cray, as this sale took place in 1781, within the period that Hasted was researching and writing his account.

On his death in 1797, Gerard asked to be buried in St Mary Cray, strengthening the conclusion that this was their family home, and Amy seems to have stayed on there, as three of their children died a few years later at St Mary Cray and are buried in the church with their father. Gerard may have intended Highcliffe Castle to be a home marking the summit of his achievements. But he died two years after its purchase at the comparatively early age of forty-six and it was sold almost immediately by Amy, along with the various other land holdings Gerard had left to her.

From this sketch of Gerard van Heythuysen's life, it seems that Higham Hall was simply a minor landholding in his investment portfolio and, indeed, figured little in his life. He sold it in 1781, probably to enable him to consolidate his fortune into more agreeable pieces of land or valuables of some other kind. It is not clear from the records who rented the Higham estate during the Van Heythuysen period of ownership, although it is unlikely that it was left empty during this long period when productive agricultural land remained a good investment for an absentee owner.

However, if the van Heythuysens saw Higham Hall and the farm only as an investment, inherited almost literally from 'country cousins', the next owners - who also originated from London, and from 'trade' - were to go back to the approach of Samuel Cordwell and Samuel Levinge and adopt Higham Hall as their country home. In doing so, they also made major changes to the nature and appearance of the house and made a determined effort to consolidate the area of farmland. The story of the Taylors of Higham Hall begins well, but as it develops, it becomes a cautionary tale of the trouble which can come from failing to make a will.

Chapter 7

John, Henry and James Taylor - the Taylors of Taylors Lane

As explained previously, Kent had a distinct system of landholding, known as *gavelkind*. As well as having consequences for the sale and size of estates, it also had consequences for their inheritance. Land in Kent could be willed but, in the absence of a will, particular rules governed how it would be inherited.

To explain this, we need to look at the changes to landholding made by the Norman Conquest. Before the Conquest, land was held in a variety of piecemeal ways across the country, depending on the prevailing customs of successive settlers and small kingdoms. In most regions, land was held by communities, individual landholders, or the local overlord (which in some areas included the Anglo-Saxon Crown). The Church was a major landholder and the main, but not the only, holder of 'bookland' (bocland tenure), that is land granted by a written charter (or entry in a book). In many areas, land was waste - not settled, not used, and in practice, not held by anyone.

By virtue of the Conquest, William I (and thus the Crown), gained possession not just of the land of the Anglo-Saxon Crown, but of all the land in the country, wasteland and all

- except for that owned by the Church. This enabled William to reward his followers and secure allegiance by the grant of land to them. Such grants adopted the Norman model of feudal tenure - whereby the land was owned by the King but granted to the holder in return for services - whether knight service or simply the right of seisin (which was a duty to pay a sum to the King when the land passed to one's heir).

This is the origin of the term freeholder, which today has come to mean owner, but originated as a term for he or she who holds the land of the king or other lord, and if held in free tenure, with no requirement of service.

Along with feudal tenure, came the custom of primogeniture, by which the oldest son or next heir in line succeeded to the freehold or other tenure, on the death of the person originally granted the land. This successor held the land as the representative of the original recipient of the land. And so, if duties such as service or money payments attached to the land, they attached to this new representative. Land was not therefore inherited but succeeded to, usually with a payment (seisin) to the lord for the privilege of succession.

The consequences of this legal structure, in most of England, were:

to encourage the development and holding of large estates of land;

to restrict the sale of land (sales of the use of land developed instead, leading to quite an extensive separation between the holder of legal title of the land and the person using it, in some cases); and

to create a cumbersome system of land conveyancing which makes reading the relevant historical documents confusing until the simple deed of conveyance was introduced by the Conveyance by Release Act 1841.

However, Kent had an unusually consistent form of customary tenure, Gavelkind, which survived as a peculiarity after 1066 and which was not abolished until 1925. Some attribute this to settlement by the Jutes in the fifth and sixth centuries whilst others to the beneficial transport links and fertile soil of the area, which reduced the need for subsistence based communal settlements. Bolton describes gavelkind as follows:

'...*a form of partible inheritance; the holding was divided among all the male heirs at death. If there was a widow, she was to have half the holding...*'[128]

Alongside this, went the liberties of being able to dispose of land by a will, to alienate (sell land) from the age of fifteen, and protection from seizure of the land (*escheating*) in the case of treason or felony.

It is an interesting question as we look at the history of the Taylor family's ownership of Higham Hall, whether, having come down from London to buy land, they failed to understand the prevailing custom of gavelkind, with consequences that caused ongoing financial problems to them and to the estate.

John Taylor

It may be helpful at this point to set out a family tree for the Taylors.

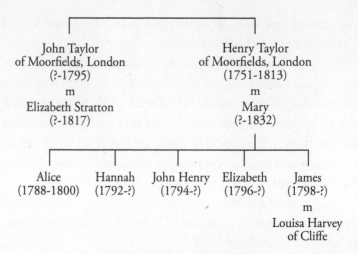

```
        John Taylor                          Henry Taylor
     of Moorfields, London               of Moorfields, London
          (?-1795)                             (1751-1813)
             m                                     m
     Elizabeth Stratton                         Mary
          (?-1817)                             (?-1832)

    Alice      Hannah    John Henry   Elizabeth     James
 (1788-1800)  (1792-?)    (1794-?)     (1796-?)    (1798-?)
                                                      m
                                                 Louisa Harvey
                                                  of Cliffe
```

Fig 9 : The Taylor Family Tree

John Taylor bought Higham Hall from the van Heythuysens in 1781. The mid-eighteenth to the early nineteenth century was a period of rising demand for agricultural produce, and a shortage of suitable land.[129] As a result, farming had to become more productive and more efficient, an imperative which was reflected in developments in stock breeding and enclosure. This style of farming suited farmsteads which stood in the middle of their own land and Higham Hall typifies that type of farm design, praised in the mid-eighteenth century as offering maximum efficiency.[130] This pattern had a barn for storage and threshing, livestock buildings, a yard for cattle in the winter, and where manure was collected. But how much of this was appreciated by the Taylors is a little hard to judge.

John Taylor and his brother Henry were clock and watch makers, with a jointly held property and business in Moorfields. A subsequent property deed records Henry, together with John's widow, Elizabeth, operating from the London address of 41 Wilson Street, Upper Moorfields, while a 1782 list made by Benjamin Vulliamy includes the Taylors of Moorfield among 286 people carrying on the trade of clock and watchmaking in London.

Having a London business and no apparent links with Higham, John Taylor may simply have bought the estate as an investment and country home. There is no evidence of any previous link between the Taylors and Higham. But although we can't tell how John Taylor originally came to know of Higham, we do know that he bought the estate in its entirety when it came up for sale in 1781. Deeds of 24 and 25 December record the sale of land

> *'including the capital messuage* known as Higham Hall, together with thirteen acres of land known as Higham Hall Farm… and including the pond orchard (three acres), and all that orchard called Winters (10 acres)'.* [131]

The feet of fine records (the eighteenth-century equivalent of a Land Registry transfer document, so called because of the monetary fine receipt attached to the bottom of a written judgment deciding title to a piece of land) lists

> *'two messuages, two cottages, four barns, ten orchards, ninety acres of land, ten acres of meadow, twenty acres of pasture, ten acres of marsh, twenty acres of wood… with the appurtenances in Higham, Chalk, Cliffe, Shorne and Frindsbury.'* [132]

---

* A capital messuage is the term used in deeds for a large residential property, usually comprising a dwelling house, outbuildings and a small area of land

All this was bought by John Taylor for £1,860 (around £160,000 in today's money). At 150 acres, it was a substantial estate, but John Taylor spent the next few years consolidating his land, buying half an acre in Hobletts, two and a half acres in Childers Hill Wood, two acres next to Winters Orchard, half an acre of woodland at the Mount (now possibly the site of the house called Mount Pleasant), three acres up to the Cherry Orchards and some further common land in 1783. Most of this was bought from a long-standing Higham family, the Prebbles, and the deed refers to the land in part as being '*Cordwell land*', suggesting it had been part of the 'original' estate, perhaps sold by the Van Heythuysen's, that John Taylor was buying back.[133] In 1785, a further four acres of salt marsh, with two cottages, were bought from the Goldsmith family. Some of the land either included existing buildings, or were built on - see the detailed descriptions in Appendix 2 - to provide accommodation to let to smallholders and market gardeners, providing the Taylors with additional income.

To begin with, Higham Hall itself was tenanted, probably by the same people Gerard van Heythuysen had leased it to. Land Tax records for Higham for the year 1780-1 suggest that Higham Hall Farm was let to an Edward Curnwdle (sic). It is possible that this man was an offshoot of the Cordwell family mis-recorded, but it is not clear from either the parish records or any other source if this was the case, or just a coincidentally similar name. From 1787-8, the farm was occupied by William Tomlin, of whom nothing is known, apart from the distressing regularity with which his infant children were buried in St Mary's - William and Elizabeth Tomlin buried Mary in August 1787, John in June 1794, Thomas in March 1801, Eleanor in

September 1803 and Edward in 1806: all of them were only weeks or months old when they died.

But the same records suggest that John Taylor and his wife Mary occupied the house themselves from 1784-86, and 1787-95, with two short periods above when the farm appears to have been let to tenant farmers. He may well have shared his country home with his brother, Henry. Certainly Henry's second daughter, Hannah, was baptised in St Mary's Church, after her birth in 1792.

At the same time, John Taylor made substantial structural changes to the house, adding a Georgian front to the southern side, and a three sided turret on to the west end. These works were completed in 1786, and changed the appearance of the house from a simple Wealden farmhouse, with perhaps two family bedrooms to a gentleman's residence with five.

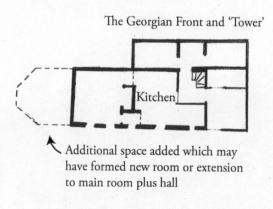

The Georgian Front and 'Tower'

Kitchen

Additional space added which may have formed new room or extension to main room plus hall

Figure 10a): Ground Floor 1786

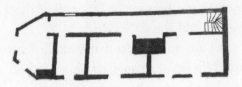

The Georgian First Floor -
two bedrooms become four

Figure 10b: First Floor 1786

The Attic Floor: the attics may already
have been in use but the new 'tower' room
had a fireplace and was suitable for a
family member

Figure 10c): Second Floor in 1786

Fig 11: The Georgian Front 1786

In October 1795, John Taylor died. He was buried in St Mary's Churchyard, on 4 November. Despite at least fourteen years of at least part time residence in Higham, he is described in the register as 'a Gentleman from London'. An inventory (Appendix 1) which was prepared in January 1796 as part of forthcoming legal proceedings (see below), gives a picture of a comfortable but not lavish eighteenth-century home, with pewter tableware, heavy wood furniture and velvet hangings in the best bedroom.

There are no records of any children being born to John and Elizabeth; John died without a will and this omission dogged the Higham Hall estate for some considerable period afterwards. It may have been John's intention that his brother Henry, then aged forty-four, should inherit the estate, hopefully with some provision for John's widow, Elizabeth. Alternatively, some agreement may have been reached to give Elizabeth the property in Moorfields. A deed of 1797 made by Henry Taylor refers to a

'...verbal agreement [by which] Mrs Taylor and myself jointly followed on the business of clock-making from October 28 1795 to August 27 1796'[134]

Whatever John's intentions had been, Elizabeth seems to have known that, the estate being in Kent, she could rely upon the custom of Gavelkind to secure more of it than her brother in law had allowed her. To establish this right, she began two years of legal dispute with Henry, a dispute which generated a number of documents held in the Kent Local History Archives.

As already suggested, it is possible that neither John nor Henry was originally aware of gavelkind. If John had died quite suddenly he would not have had time to take the legal advice he needed to provide the succession he wanted for his estate. What may have seemed a pragmatic solution - Henry to have the Higham estate, with Henry and Elizabeth sharing the London house and building, was not in fact 'legal', as the custom of gavelkind entitled a widow with no children to half of the whole estate as a tenant for life. The upshot of the proceedings (in the end decided by arbitration rather than a court case) was that the value of all of John Taylor's chattels and moveable possessions, in Kent and in London, had to be valued and divided between Henry and Elizabeth.

The bitterness that this process caused is obvious from Henry's assertion in the 1797 deed that while he and Elizabeth were jointly in business

> *'she took most of the income from this period... 'withholding money [which] prevented me from undertaking a large order for Russia... there was a considerable quantity of red port in the London house to which she gave me no account'* [135]

He goes on to accuse her of taking plate and other goods before the inventory was taken from the house in London. The valuation concluded that

> *'the said stock of implements of husbandry, cattle, and other property in and about the farm [in Higham] were on or about the 28th of December then appraised and valued by George Gunning and Philip Boghurst esquires at the sum of £1062, 14 shillings and six pence, and the said household goods were then appraised by them at the*

sum of £90, sixteen shillings and sixpence, and the said
stock in trade implements and utensils in and about the
said premises on Wilson street were on or about 26 August
last appraised or valued by Robert Wood and William
Dorrell clockmakers at the sum of £1203 18 shillings and
5 pence... which made together £2407 nine shillings and
five pence...'

Other, minor adjustments must have been made to these sums, as the arbitrators concluded that

' and given that Elizabeth Taylor and Henry Taylor are
entitled to equal shares, Henry Taylor stood indebted to
Elizabeth Taylor £1111' [136]

In addition, Elizabeth was owed an annual payment of £63 and 5 shillings from the profits of the estate, as a life tenant under gavelkind.

One can imagine, even at this distance in time, that by the conclusion of the dispute, Henry was determined not to sell any of his share of the estate, or to release any of it to Elizabeth. Instead, his wish was to settle with her financially and to reduce his dealings with her to a minimum. Unfortunately, not having £1111 to hand, and unwilling to raise it by other means, Henry accepted a charge on the Higham Hall estate, in favour of his sister in law, which then dominated the economics of the estate for the next forty years.

For now, Henry appears to have settled in to Higham Hall, with his own wife Mary, two sons, John Henry and James, and three daughters, Alice, Elizabeth and Hannah. Land Tax records put him in occupation from 1796 to 1813. With Higham Hall extended as it had been to a four to six bedroomed property by his brother John, Henry's family could have been comfortably accommodated in the house. His will, written just before his death at the age of sixty-three, refers to the London house in Horse Shoe Alley, Moorfields, being let out to a Mr Thornton or Thorn, which supports the view that at this point in time, Higham Hall was the family's main home.

Like John, Henry seems to have had some involvement with the village. On 10 April 1807 he was elected one of the trustees of Rolfe's charity (a local charitable foundation), although he is only recorded as having attended one meeting, in April 1809. He was a little more conscientious in his attendance at vestry meetings (the forerunner of the parish council).[137] He also appears to have continued John's efforts to expand the estate, buying land around Dusty Hill (in the Two Gates Hill area) from the Roper Head family at the Hermitage, in 1795. [138] It may have been Henry who gave the family name to Taylors Lane - although this is not recorded anywhere.*

The inventories and valuations done during the course of the legal dispute provide a useful picture of the condition of the estate at this time. The stock, crops and equipment on the farm were listed as follows:

'Stock in the yard - two waggons, three carts, two small carts, 1 light cart, one water barrel and carriage.
3 fatting hogs, 2 small pigs, hog hutch and three troughs.
Four small pigs. One sow and seven pigs. One sow.
Ten heifers and 2 cows.

* Apart from one earlier reference to Higham Hill Lane, the road is always called Taylors Lane in the sources available, which all date from after the Taylors' period in residence

1 riding mare 6 years old; one riding mare aged; one cart horse, aged; one cart colt, two years old; one cart horse colt 1 year old; one horse trough

In the stable - one gelding 'Poppet', ten years old; one gelding 'Bowler', 4 years; one gelding 'Gilbert, sixteen years; one gelding 'Lion, fifteen years; one mare 'White Hoof', ten years; one mare 'Jolly', twenty years old.

One plough compleat for six horses and harness; five chain harness and bits; 3 pair rugs and quilters; six old collars; 2 corn chests; a pair of old chains; a new saddle with plated stirrups and two bridles; three dung forks, two shovels and two chaff baskets;

In the granary - a quantity of wool; fifty quarter of sacks; eight pitch forks; one sack barrows; eight pair of traces and one hundredwgt of oil cake; 1 hundredweight of rope yarns; two ladders; a seed basket and flatters; a pair of wagon ropes; a timber chain; and 3 skid chains

In the barn - 3 hives; 1 skippet; two shovels; two bushels; Stack yard - 3 stack frames; nine stones each; one old plough for broad sharing; one new plough for striking barley; one new plough for beans; one new plough for wheat; one pair of wheat harrows; two brakes and one foot plough; a wheel; four elm sheep troughs; two old ploughs and old roll; six sheep racks; one hundred and forty hurdle gates; one pair of ox harrows;

Sheep - 48 new ewes; twenty nine old ewes; and twenty one wethers

Crops sown - wheat 42 acres ,Rye 5 acres, Seeds 12 acres, Fallow 5 acres, Rape 7 acres' [139]

Apart from the sheep and the crops, the clear picture is of a working farm, with a number of animals kept in the farm buildings and yard across from the house and the usual jumble of farm equipment scattered throughout the barns and sheds. The valuers commented that the farm needed at least £150 to be spent on maintenance to put it in a proper state of repair and to make it fit for renting out. This was perhaps a reflection of the Van Heythuysen's previous lack of interest in the property and the productivity of its tenants, combined with the Taylors' inexperience of farming and country life.

The stock in Wilson Street, Moorfields comprised around sixty clocks, and were valued more highly than the farm contents - despite Elizabeth's alleged removal of the plate and the port wine.

Henry died some sixteen years later, on 9 April 1813 and was buried in St Mary's Church. After his own experience, he was careful to leave a will, even if this did not quite reflect the wishes of his family as it was drafted. Henry is described as 'gent' in the burials register. His will left the entire estate to his wife, Mary, for her life, with the London property passing to their younger son, James, on her death, and the Higham properties to their oldest son, John Henry, with five hundred pounds apiece to his two surviving daughters (Alice had died in 1800, at the age of twelve). Henry's *dear friend* and London neighbour, James Watts, was appointed the executor, along with Mary. The London properties bequeathed to James Taylor at this point were valued at £970 (£84,000 today), and let to Mr Thornton still.

However, it is clear from other documents in the archive that at this point, Elizabeth's charge on the property had not been paid up. When Elizabeth herself died in September 1817, her charge was inherited by her brother, Matthias Stratton. In a rather sad extract from later legal documents it is recorded that:

'*And reciting that Matthias Stratton called in this sum from Mary Taylor, and they not having sufficient monies or effects, James Watts agreed to pay off the mortgage with the house as security.*' [140]

So the charge was paid up after Elizabeth's death, but only by Henry's wife and sons obtaining a mortgage on Higham Hall from Henry's executor, James Watts. Mary must have hoped that James would be a better creditor than her sister in law, but unfortunately, James Watts himself died intestate in 1818 (a year after taking the mortgage on Higham Hall). Although the deeds record that John Henry and Mary Taylor paid off the sum of £1111 to James Watts's executors, with the aim of freeing the property from all encumbrances, this did not prove to be the case, and, there were further complications for the Taylors nearly twenty years later. Some small pieces of the estate appear to have been sold off to finance this.

It seems likely that initially after Henry's death, Mary Taylor let the house and farm. More details of this are set out in Chapter 8, but four years into Mary's widowhood, in 1817, tenants by the name of Gates are recorded as being in residence. By now the settlement with her sister in law, Elizabeth, has been made, and the mortgage obtained, and it may have been felt that the property needed to generate more income to repay the debts incurred to keep it. Mary moved back into Higham Hall, after the Gates' tenancy, between 1823 and 1825. Then after this, in 1826, Mary's younger son, James, moved into Higham Hall Farm and began to run the estate himself. [141] By this time, James was in his late twenties and presumably felt able to take on the task.

In August 1832, Mary Taylor died in Gravesend, where she appears to have been living. She was buried on 24 August 1832 in St Mary's Church Higham, and the two properties Henry Taylor had owned passed in accordance with his will; the Higham Hall estate to the eldest son, John Henry Taylor, and the London property to James Taylor.

Unfortunately, this division of property did not seem to suit John Henry and James' personal interests and circumstances. After all, at this point, James had already been occupying and running the estate for six years. So, within two years of their mother's death, the brothers had effectively exchanged their legacies, with James Taylor buying Higham Hall and parts of the related estate from his older brother in January 1834. James had raised the cash for this purchase by mortgaging the London house to a London Tea Merchant called Edward Eagleton - of whom we will hear more later. At the time of the sale, the estate was described as:

> *Those several pieces of land containing together by estimation thirteen acres of the estate called Higham Hall farm described in lease of 1781 called the Pond Orchard, containing three acres and all that orchard called Winters containing 10 acres... All those pieces of land together by estimation 16 acres 2 roods of the said estate called Higham Hall Farm... described as half an acre lying and being in Hobletts... and the parcel of land comprising half an acre and being in the ground formerly of Madam Elinor Cordwell widow deceased but then of John Taylor,*

*adjoining to the woods… and 2 and a half acres of wood-
land in Childers Hill Wood and one acre of land lying
in Winters… Two acres under Winters heading up to
Masons and the 8 acres in turf and the five yards left
in the common field adjoining to the ground owned by
Madam Cordwell then John Taylor and the three acres up
to the cherry ground and half an acre of woodland called
The Mount.*

*Altogether 16 acres, all in the parish of Higham [which
were] lately in the occupation of John Prebble and then
in the tenure or occupation of John Taylor or his heirs…
land on Higham Common forming part of the estate of
Higham Hall farm [which]… includes 4 acres of salt
marsh formerly held by William Smith and then Henry
Masters, with 2 houses held by Thomas French and Louis
Blacksmith… Marshland occupied or tenanted by John
and Thomas Goldsmith*

*Fourthly 17 acres of land, part of the Higham Hall estate
… including Dusty Hill, Two Gates field, Hobletts,
Hobletts Common field, Northcroft in Higham and all
messuages and land which Henry Taylor died seized of in
Higham, Cliffe, Chalk, Shorne and Frindsbury.'* [142]

Although not all of these areas and field names can be identified from a modern map of Higham, some (such as Childrens
Hill Wood) can, and what is interesting is the cumulative
description of land holding. Although I have omitted the dates,
the descriptions refer back to lease and title deeds of previous
owners. These describe parcels of land which - rather than
relying on the precisely drawn plans of the Land Registry today

- refer to land as 'that formerly held by Madam Cordwell', even though at the time of writing this deed of conveyance, Eleanor Cordwell had been dead for 125 years.

Although the sources in the County Archives describe this transfer of ownership between John Henry Taylor and James Taylor, we do not know a great deal about them. Throughout the references, John Henry is described as being a gentleman, and usually described as residing in or near the Strand in London. There is no evidence of any sort to link him to Higham, beyond these land transactions, and his baptism in St Marys Church in August 1807, at the age of thirteen. (For some reason, three of Henry and Mary's four surviving children - John Henry born 1794, Elizabeth born 1796 and James born 1798 - were baptised, or, more likely, re-baptised, in Higham in 1807.) It seems clear from what records we have that John Henry preferred an urban life and pursuits - in which case he would have been pleased by the conversion of his inheritance into ready cash.

James Taylor, on the other hand, is variously recorded as living in Borstal (Rochester), Milton (Gravesend), Penenden Heath (Maidstone), and finally in Withyham, Sussex. He is described as either a farmer or a miller, and only once as a gentleman. He is possibly the same James Taylor who married a local woman - Louisa Harvey from Cliffe in 1828 - he would then have been thirty. However, his presumed efforts to establish himself as a landed farmer seem to have been a constant struggle, marked by the need to borrow money against the estate, a situation which was not helped by the liabilities of gavelkind tenure again intervening. From the time of his mother's death - perhaps as an effort to get it to produce more and to establish a regular income - he appears to have let out the house and farm (see chapter 8 below).

Despite being relieved of the practicalities of farming, James spent the next eleven years engaged in a series of legal disputes and financial transactions concerning the estate. For example, a year after James bought the estate from his brother, he was subject to a lawsuit from the heirs and executors of his uncle, James Watts. They argued that despite the fact that James Watts's mortgage had been bought out by John Henry and Mary Taylor in 1818, their right to inherit part of the estate under gavelkind (even if it had only been held as security) entitled them to a payment from James. The deeds do not reveal how much that liability was, but they do show that James borrowed against the estate on a number of occasions - £350 in 1823 (when it was still owned by his mother), £300 in 1832, and £500 in 1834.

As part of the deal to buy the estate from his older brother, James undertook to pay John Henry £25 quit rent annually, and to take on the liability for his sisters' legacies - some £500 each. That he had difficulty paying these (as well as the mortgages on the property) is shown by the later lawsuit brought against him by his sister Elizabeth and her children in June 1843.

Just a year after the Watts' lawsuit, in 1836, James became embroiled in a case against his lawyer- the case of Taylor v Blacklow which reinforces the important principle that *the first duty of an attorney is to keep the secrets of his client* (Gaselee J). The case arose when James engaged Blacklow as his attorney, to arrange a mortgage of £4000 against Higham Hall. In the course of his work, Blacklow noticed that James' title to the estate was defective in some parts, because the land had been inaccurately measured and recorded in the indentures. Despite his duties to James, Blacklow reported this find back to John Henry Taylor, and assisted John Henry to bring a number of suits of eviction and recovery of timber from the pieces of land with the defective title. Although these actions were themselves defeated and the case against Blacklow proved in the House of Lords, the whole affair involved James in a further year of litigation, and the loss of £2000, which neither his brother nor his attorney could pay back to him. [143]

When James' unequal struggle came to a head in 1836, he was forced to borrow a total of £6,300 (rather than the intended £4000) from Edward Eagleton, the merchant he had sold the London house in Moorfields to only two years earlier. This sum (approx. £480,000 today) was secured against 154 acres of land, including Higham Hall itself, let to the Barnes family of Higham for £120 a year, and the farm, let to the same family for £250 per year. Again, James appears to have been unable to keep up the payments on the mortgage - Edward Eagleton's loan was consolidated to £10,350 secured against all of the estate, including the holdings in Kent, Sussex and Middlesex. But James' finances did not recover and ultimately, Edward Eagleton foreclosed on the loan and took ownership of the estate.

Even before he lost the estate, James appears to have retired to a property in Sussex, presumably smaller and cheaper to run, where he is described as a gentleman, rather than as a farmer. He is not buried in Higham, and from this point on, the Taylors cease to figure in Higham's story. Despite their name being a permanent part of Higham's landscape and their impact on the outward appearance of Higham Hall, their sixty-two years of ownership appear as perhaps an example of the risks of investing in areas outside one's knowledge and skills. It ushered in a sixty year period of tenant farming on the estate.

Chapter 8

Tenant farmers

We saw in the previous chapter that after John Taylor's death, Mary began to rent out the house and land. George and Phyliss Gates and their large family moved in at some point between 1814 and 1817 - having left Combe Farm in Hoo - an area described as marshy land between the highway and river. After this more marginal land, Higham Hall was presumably an improvement, despite its dilapidated state. [144] The Gates' tenth child, Elizabeth, was baptised from Higham Hall on 17 July 1817 and Thomas, their eleventh, two years later. But subsequent census evidence shows that the family as a whole did not gain a lot from their period of residence - as adults, the Gates children became a boot and shoemaker, a dressmaker and the wife of an undertaker, retaining a consistent status as lower ranking trades people.

After the Gates' tenancy, Mary, and subsequently James Taylor, moved back into Higham Hall and farmed the land directly. By the 1830s, as James' efforts ran into increasing problems, the farm and house were let again - this time to William Barnes and his family.

Parish records suggest that William Barnes was born in Hoo in 1801. He married Ann Akhurst from Higham in October 1825, and the fact that she entered her mark onto the marriage register, rather than signing her name, suggests that she at least came from modest circumstances. A year later, their first child, Ann, was born, at which time William is described as a gardener, living at Gore Green in Higham - although this is likely to have meant market gardening, rather than maintaining a garden for someone else. Two sons followed - William in 1828 and James in 1829 - while William senior appears to have been building up his market gardening business. (As was noted in Chapter 1, this was a period of expansion in the growth of vegetables and fruit in the area, owing to improvements in transport and ready markets in London).[145]

William's first wife, Ann, died in 1830 and William's second marriage five years later seems a rather grander affair. He married Sarah Snelling from Meopham and oddly the wedding took place in St Paul's Church, Covent Garden. William was thirty-four, with three young children, and his second wife was just nineteen.

William and Sarah's life together at Higham Hall began in 1831/32. William is named as the tenant of Mary Taylor in the 1832 Land Tax Record, succeeding James Taylor (see previous chapter). William next appears in the vestry meeting register from 1840, illustrating that he was becoming prominent in Higham's small society. In the 1841 Tithe Schedule, he is confirmed as renting Higham Hall together with the bulk of the rest of the Higham Hall estate - totalling seventy acres - from James Taylor. The land included forty-six acres of arable, six acres of plantation (presumably fruit trees), more than five acres of pasture on the saltings and the acre making up the farmstead itself. The same schedule lists nine other lots of land rented out by James.

So, within six years of his second marriage, William had become a substantial tenant farmer, living in a comfortable six bedroomed farmhouse, employing two labourers and a house servant. The census of this same year (1841) records that as well as William and Sarah and the fifteen-year-old Ann, the Barnes family had expanded to include three more children - Emily (four), Thomas (three) and Frederick (one).

William's older boys were boarded out at school in Strood at this point, which was probably just as well in terms of space, as Sarah Barnes continued to have children at roughly two-year intervals, until Alice, their last was born in 1857. Although Sarah's first child, Emily, died in 1844 at the age of seven, her other ten children all survived, leaving William the father of thirteen surviving children by his death in 1859.* This is not untypical of Victorian families - medical, hygiene and nutritional advances having made it more likely that parents would bring their children to maturity.

The fact that a number of the Barnes children spent some period of their lives being educated at small local schools lends support to the idea that William was earning enough revenue from his farmlands and, particularly, his orchards, to support a decent lifestyle for his family. (see Appendix 2 for more detail on the types of land rented by William, and the annual rents he could afford to pay). More than that, William became part of the village establishment during his lifetime. From a market gardener in a small house, he established himself as a regular attender at vestry meetings and he was evidently literate and

---

*   Emily Barnes is buried with her parents in St Mary's Church, Higham. Her epitath reads 'Nipp'd in the Bud, so Beautiful and Good, Her Blessed Spirit now rests with God'

numerate. In 1845 he was elected to the office of parish overseer - responsible for collecting and paying out relief to the poor. He retained this position until his death fourteen years later.

William was clearly never considered a gentleman, however. The 1851 Post Office Directory, for example, lists William under 'Traders', with only four men (including the vicar) listed as 'Gentry'. Similarly, Bagshaw's Directory (1847 edition) lists only Great Hermitage and Mockbeggar as 'residences of note' in Higham, not Higham Hall.

Despite this, the Barnes family would have been a relatively prominent family in the village. In the 1850s, Kelly's Directory records a population of 843 people living in Higham, 68% of them were engaged in agriculture or labouring. Andrew Rootes describes the village as one of *fields and orchard, trees and hedge-rows...* 'with hamlets at Church Street, Chequers Street, Gore Green and Upper Higham. [146] There was no building around Mid-Higham (currently where the The Gardeners Arms and Post Office are), at this time.

William rented Higham Hall and the estate from around 1831 to 1859, nearly thirty years in total. The stability and relative prosperity of his tenancy was no doubt of considerable benefit to the management of the estate, after James Taylor's struggles, and William was able to expand his holding over time. By 1851 he rented 110 acres and employed nine men and two women, while Sarah had two house servants to help with her increasingly large household.

During this period, however, fifteen year old Sophia Wilkins, from Gore Green, is recorded, quite baldly, in the parish registers as dying at Higham Hall '*of smallpox* [perhaps more accurately sepsis in this case], *after being burned*'. This was reported a good deal more sensationally in the newspapers:

'Death By Burning - Died on Sunday afternoon, at the residence of Mr Barnes, Higham Hall, near Rochester, a young woman named Wilkins, who was there as a visitor. It appears that a few days before her death, the deceased was watching a saucepan containing some potatoes, which was boiling over the fire for dinner, when by some accident some of her dress caught fire; so rapid were the flames, that although Mr Barnes was close at hand and procured a blanket, which he wrapped around her, the poor woman's body was most dreadfully burnt… The poor creature whilst she lived suffered dreadfully.' [147]

Perhaps Sophia was a friend of Ann Barnes but her ghastly death did not put the family off from remaining at Higham Hall. As an aside, it suggests that in this comparatively late time, cooking was being done in the house over an open fire, in an inglenook, rather than on a fitted range or stove. Given the number of young children in the Barnes household, it is perhaps surprising that more events of this kind were not recorded. It illustrates perhaps that William and Sarah's improving efforts were restricted to the farm and that the house itself remained in need of updating.

Sarah's two servants brought the usual number of occupants of the house to twelve. The 1851 census, for example, lists the occupants as William and Sarah, William's two older sons (William and James) in their early twenties, six of Sarah's children, ranging in age from ten to seven months, and two house servants, Sarah aged twenty-one and Mercy, aged fifteen. Thomas, then aged twelve, was boarding at school in

Gravesend, which relieved the demand for rooms a little. By using the garret rooms though, as the servants and children undoubtedly did, the house had eight bedrooms to accommodate the sixteen inhabitants who may have lived there during holiday times (see the plans at pages 99 & 100 above).

That Higham Hall provided a comfortable living and growing prosperity for the Barnes family is suggested by the married lives of their children. While Edward (William's fifth son) stayed on to farm in Higham, William junior, James and Thomas all became farmers in their own right on the Hoo peninsula, returning to the area of their father's birth. Given that William originally came to Higham as a market gardener on a small scale, it seems likely that the three boys needed to buy or rent land, presumably with their parent's help to get started, rather than moving on to established family farms. (There is some evidence of money left by their mother's Akehurst family to the oldest two boys, which may have helped them out a little.)[148] This would have required William and Sarah to have some capital to give or lend them, at least to begin with.

William and Sarah's fourth daughter, Albina, married a grocer's clerk merchant and was well off enough at the end of her life to live in an apartment in central Brighton on her own independent means. Another daughter, Harriet, married into an established farming family in Meopham, and her father in law, John French is described as a gentleman on the marriage certificate. Perhaps the best example is the marriage of William's eldest daughter, Ann. At the age of nineteen, she married a tobacconist from Maidstone, Richard Doe, who progressed to becoming a local councillor, JP and the Mayor of Maidstone for a period.

None of this is probative, but, taken together, it paints the picture of an aspirational and improving family, whose increased prosperity and status was based upon a thriving farm. Ann's mother, William's first wife, had been unable to sign her name on her marriage, but her family, and William's later children, all of whom attended school, seem to have moved on considerably from then.

When William died in 1859, he left Sarah a widow of forty-three, with seven children under sixteen to care for (Edward 14, Sarah 12, Albina 10, Esther 8, Walter 6, Arthur 4 and Alice only 2). Higham Hall was almost immediately advertised as available to let, but it not clear whether this was provoked by Sarah's wish to move out or decided for her by her landlord, Edward Eagleton (see Chapter 9 below). The advert in the Eastern Gazette dated 22 November 1859 offered Higham Hall Farm (fifty-five acres of good sound productive land, including a comfortable residence) to be let on lease with immediate possession.

Possibly Sarah had negotiated a smaller estate for herself - she moved to New House Farm - now known as Hill Farm - further up Taylors Lane. Given that the Higham Hall estate had apparently shrunk in size, she may have begun by renting a smaller section of it. Nonetheless, just two years later she is recorded in the 1861 census as farming an estate of 100 acres, employing five men and four boys. In 1871, she was farming the same land, but now 115 acres, and employing seven men, three boys and three women.

Both Albina and Alice had periods at school in Rochester, which would need to be paid for. Whilst her son Edward was evidently helping Sarah with the farm at some point and to some extent (he is described as the farmer at New House Farm in a trade directory of 1867), both census entries record Sarah as the head of household, and by 1871 Edward had his own farm in Higham, with only sixteen-year-old Arthur still at home.

We don't know who Sarah rented this land from - it is possible that this was a section or sections of the larger Higham Hall estate broken up in 1843 (see for example, Lot 19 in Appendix 2, and page 125 below). But it seems clear that someone considered her to be to be a viable tenant and a good farmer. Sarah remained at New House Farm until the late 1870s, dying in 1880, and leaving £2000 in her will (£130,000 today).

The Barnes' success and long tenure at Higham Hall was not repeated, and subsequent tenants, with much smaller families and shorter periods of tenure seem not to have made so much progress. In 1861, two years after the death of William Barnes, William and Anne Tompsett, a couple in their late twenties, with two sons, William and Frank, aged two and three, became tenants. A daughter, Anna, was later born at Higham Hall.

William is described as a farmer and market gardener - perhaps reflecting a shift in the use of the land from arable to fruit growing. He was at this point farming fifty acres and he employed three boys and two women, together with one house servant, Harriet Bodkin. William and Anne Tompsett had moved from the Maidstone area, where William's father worked as an auctioner and appraiser. William's father left him less than £300 on his death in 1864 and so it appears that the Tompsetts were of lesser means than the Barnes family - although they perhaps lived in greater comfort in the house given that they had considerably fewer children to fit in. But around the time of his father's death, William appears to have taken on his practice, and by 1867, William Tompsett, though still living in Higham, is described simply as an auctioneer. By 1899 a letter to the Maidstone and Kentish Journal (about Charles Dickens' involvement in the Staplehurst railway accident) shows that the Tompsetts were living in Tonbridge.

The 1871 census records that William and Elizabeth Fuller (aged forty-seven and fifty-two) were living in the house. They are described as farming sixty acres, and employing five men, one boy and two house servants, Charlotte Theobald and William Taylor. While there is no specific evidence as to whether or not the Fullers owned the house and land, this seems unlikely. Ten years later (1881) they are described as market gardeners of twelve acres, living in Canal Cottage in Higham, a much less salubrious address, although they still employed two men and one boy to work the land.

Again, it is not clear exactly when the Fullers left Higham Hall, but they were the last set of tenant farmers to rent it, as, sometime between 1871 and 1874, the house and estate were let to a very different kind of tenant, Vitale de Michele. Vitale represented a return to the kind of incomer we saw one hundred years previously, when John Taylor bought the house and determined to live in it.

But having looked at the tenants, before we move on to the story of Vitale and his family, we should return briefly to the owners of the house in the period from James Taylor in the mid nineteenth century, to Thomas Whitebread fifty years later.

Chapter 9

Nineteenth-century owners and landlords

At the end of Chapter 7, we saw that Edward Eagleton became the owner of Higham Hall. This appears to have taken place at some point between 1836 and 1843, as a result of James' inability to service the increasing amount of debt secured against the estate. Edward Eagleton came to know James Taylor in 1834, when James either mortgaged or sold the property in Half Moon Street, Moorfields, to buy out his older brother, John Henry Taylor, from the Higham Hall estate. Edward lent him the money to do this.

Edward Eagleton was a tea merchant in his thirties, based in Cornhill, only half a mile from Moorfields. Born in 1786, Edward had an early introduction to trade after the death of his father; by 1799 (aged thirteen) he is recorded as being in business, jointly with his mother, owning a tea warehouse called 'The Grasshopper' in Bishopsgate. His father, also Edward, has been described as

> 'One of the most interesting and earliest entrepreneurs...
> an old established London dealer... no petty dealer, in July
> 1784, he had in stock 2,359 pounds of tea' [149]

In a letter fulsomely praising William Pitt, Edward Eagleton Senior argued for Free Trade and particularly the breaking of the East India Company's stranglehold on imports. He was one of the first dealers to advertise extensively, developing a mail order business with both retail customers and small shopkeepers. He sought to act as a wholesaler, interposing himself between the East India Company (who only sold in whole lots) and shopkeepers who wanted to buy by the pound, adding only a 1% mark up for his pains. By 1793, Eagleton claimed to have twenty-seven outlets in towns and cities across England, Wales and Scotland, with his teas *packed and marked with the sign of the Grasshopper* which attached a novel element of branding to the product. [150]

His son (the Edward Eagleton who became the owner of Higham Hall) is described in one history of the City of London as *the ideal type of the mid-century city gentleman* and in his obituary as someone who *'...overcame the disadvantages of a defective education'* (presumably because he was working from the age of thirteen), *'and delicate health ... to hand over a competent fortune to his [own] sons.'* [151]

Edward junior married Ann Thornton of Westminster in 1809, and the couple had seven children born to them between 1811 and 1826. During the same period, Edward served on the Common Council of the City of London and, by 1841, the family had amassed enough wealth to move to one of the smart eighteenth-century terraced townhouses overlooking Blackheath, where Edward lived until his death in 1861. Although Edward had retired from business on 1854, handing it on to his sons, John Henry and Edward, he left an estate worth nearly £35,000 to his family (over £2 million today).

There is no evidence that Edward was anything other than an absentee owner of Higham Hall and his ownership may have been involuntary. Edward's life and career were wholly London centric and it appears to be simply because he had spare cash to invest that he became the mortgagor and then owner of Higham Hall during the 1830s. Despite his accidental ownership, one permanent record of Edward appears to remain at Higham Hall in the form of a small stone block which sits in the garden to this day, carved with the initials E E - initials that belong to no other owner of the house and which have no other obvious explanation.

By the time the estate was put up for sale by Eagleton in May 1843, it comprised 154 acres and was let to the Barnes family - described as *'most respectable tenants'*. It seems likely that the land was being sold because Eagleton had called in his loans; but it is noteworthy that the estate had grown in size since James Taylor had bought the land from his older brother. It seems unlikely that James could have bought additional land with the financial problems he had but perhaps Edward Eagleton had begun to add parcels of land to the estate as and when they came on the market. Either way, in 1843, the strategy chosen was to break the estate up into separate lots. These included orchards, fields , saltings, and one public house - the Malt Shovel in Canal Road (see Appendix 2 for more detail). Higham Hall itself was described as *'relics of the celebrated ancient mansion... converted into farming residences'*, which seems a rather misleading description and perhaps suggests that estate agents hyperbole is not a new phenomenon. It does confirm perhaps, though, that the house itself was not in a particularly good condition.

The full description emphasises the earning potential of the farm :

'the Higham Hall Estate, an Extensive and peculiarly Valuable freehold landed property. Most desirably situate in and around the pleasing Village of Higham, within the compass of a Mile and a Half of the Falstaff Hotel, at Gad's Hill, about Four Miles from Gravesend and Three from Rochester

In a rich district of the County of Kent, Intersected by the Thames & Medway Canal, Which for the conveyance of Fruit, Agricultural Produce and Manure, offers singular advantages for Horticultural and farming Operations, comprising altogether 154 acres and 22 perches, Disposed in highly productive Orchards, market gardens, detached lands, Dwelling Houses and Cottages, with numerous fine Sites for building on the North and Elevated side of the Thames' [152]

The auction was set for Friday 23 June 1843, at noon, at the Auction Mart in Bartholomew Lane, London. The twenty-six lots are listed in full in Appendix 2 and the details show the extent of the estate at this point, including a cottage and market garden in Two Gates Hill, a barn, shed and land at Dusty Hill, land between Church Street and Brick House (now Whitehouse) Farm, a double cottage and other pieces of land by the Chequers Public House, the Malt Shovel Beer Shop (formerly the Parish Work-house, apparently), woods and saltings, various arable fields, and an Orchard and Market Garden in Chalk.

It is clear that, despite John Taylor's efforts to create a gentleman's residence with its attractive Georgian frontage and turreted additions, the estate, its houses and cottages were working dwellings and family homes, rather than genteel accommodation. As much space is given in the description to the farm and other outbuildings as to the house and its living accommodation.

The details indicate that some of the land (the Filbert orchard and part of the Six Acre Field) was let to William Easdown, although the bulk of the estate was let to William Barnes, in particular, Lots 14 and 15, which made up the 'farmhouse' i.e. Higham Hall itself and its associated buildings. These are described as

> *'Commanding an elevated and very agreeable situation, in the Parish of Higham, adapted for a respectable moderate sized Family and containing*
> *Three Attics, Four Family Bedchambers, Two neat Parlours, a Kitchen, Scullery and Pantry, a Large Court Yard, Brewhouse with Loft over, Stable, Chaise House, an excellent Walled Garden, very abundantly stocked with Productive Fruit Trees, and Outer Garden or Shrubbery, and Plantation. A Farm yard, Team Stable for Five Horses, Barn, Cart Lodge and Granary. '*

The copy of the sale particulars includes a handwritten note to the effect that Lot 14, belonging to Edward Eagleton, Higham Hall, was not sold and it seems likely that Lot 15 was also unsold. Presumably, some at least of the separate lots of outlying land were sold - which would explain the availability of neighbouring land available for Sarah Barnes to rent on her husband's death in 1859 (see page 120 above). Certainly, the estate is described as a smaller acreage when leased out in 1859 than it was when for sale in 1843. There is also a date (1814) beneath the note, but this is not consistent with any of the other documents I have seen and discussed in chapter 7, so I can only presume that this was a mistake rather than being evidence that Edward had owned the land since that date.

It appears that following the failure of the sale, Edward retained the house and main farm buildings, and continued to let them to the Barnes family, and the other tenants described previously in Chapter 8.

Further attempts were made to sell the house in 1863 and 1864 - probably by the executors of Edward Eagleton, following his death in 1861. The description was a little more business-like on this occasion, although it was still described as an '*ancient residence*', with three bedrooms, a nursery, three attics, two parlours, a kitchen, wash-house and dairy, and refers to an estate of fifty acres. Both auction and private treaty were tried, but were unsuccessful.

It is not clear exactly when the house and estate were eventually sold, but records show that by the late 1870s/early 1880s Thomas Whitebread was the owner. One hopes that Edward's executors did not have to spend all this time (potentially ten to twenty years) trying to sell - but there is no evidence to clarify this either way. In 1882, the house is recorded as having a rateable value of £38 10s; the land and cottages being valued at £157 10s. In present day terms, this represents £2,515 and £10,390 respectively.

The Whitebreads are a local family, who still live in the Higham, Cliffe and Hoo areas. Thomas William Whitebread was born in 1814 in Chatham. Thomas married Jemima Harrall, from another Hoo farming family, on the 12 January 1843, in Higham. To begin with, the family lived at Randall

Bottom in Shorne, on the edge of the Cobham Hall estate, but by 1861, Thomas and Jemima were farming 200 acres at Blacklands Farm in Frindsbury - which can still be seen just off the Mockbeggar (Higham) - Wainscott Road, for those who live locally. At this point Thomas was obviously doing well, farming 200 acres and employing eight men and three boys. Their family had grown steadily, with Rosina (1851) born in Shorne and then George (1855), Alfred (1857), James (1859) and Ellen (1864) all born at the Frindsbury farm.

Thomas appears to have bought Higham Hall as an invest-ment. Certainly there is no record of him or his family living in the house. He was the owner from around the late 1870s/early 1880s, and Higham Hall seems to have been bought at the time of a general rearrangement of the Whitebreads' affairs. As well as buying Higham Hall, Thomas and Jemima left Blacklands Farm and moved into Dairy House Farm in Higham. Blacklands itself was occupied by a farm labourer and his family, which suggests that Thomas remained the owner - unless he sold it to another investor. Although Thomas and Jemima's oldest son was now in his thirties and married with children himself, he lived in a second Frindsbury prop-erty, Greenfield House, and worked as a market gardener, so Blacklands did not need to be passed on down the family. On his death, Thomas was described as farmer, market gardener and salesman, and as 'of Higham and Covent Garden', suggest-ing that he was a substantial trader in produce grown locally and sold in London.

All this suggests that the Whitebreads were quite a wealthy farming family, and this is supported by the stained glass window in St Mary's Church Higham, commissioned by

Ellen Whitebread (subsequently Blake) to commemorate her parents, her brothers and her sister. However, they also seem to have been a hard working and frugal family - all the census entries record Jemima as only having one house servant, despite homes such as Dairy House Farm being substantial properties to keep up.

We don't know any more about the Whitebreads' relationship with Higham Hall, save to say that Thomas rented the house and the estate to our next significant family, the de Michele's, and that after his death in 1890, Thomas's executors, Jemima and their son Thomas, sold the house to Vitale de Michele, to whom we turn now.

Chapter 10

The de Michele family

Visitors to Higham might wonder at the name of the row of council-built houses in Lower Higham which lie between the railway line and the old boundaries of the Higham Hall estate. 'Michele Cottages' appear to be mis-spelt, until one realises they are properly pronounced '*Mikaylee*' and commemorate a Venetian family name, rather than being the French name Michelle. The name refers to Vitale de Michele.

Vitale himself spent some time trying to trace his own origins back to the de Michele family of Venice. For our purposes, however, his immediate family background is interesting enough and presents a clear picture of the opportunities and stresses of life for upper middle class families in the late nineteenth and early twentieth century.[153]

The de Michele family lived originally in London and latterly in Surrey. Vitale's parents were prominent in nineteenth-century London society. His father, Charles Eastland de Michele, was a diplomat serving in St Petersburg from 1849 to 1866, having previously been the editor of '*The Morning Post*' newspaper. Although having an Italian grandfather, Charles was brought up in England. He married Mary Llewellyn in 1835, and they had four sons and four daughters - Mary Blanche (1836), Isabel Susan (1838), Charles Llewellyn (1839), Cyril

Troughton Stepney (1841), Nina (1843), Leopold John (1845), Carlotta Luisa (1847) and lastly, Vitale Domenico, born on 11 November 1848.

Charles Eastland was a friend of Napoleon III and his youngest daughter Carlotta was said to be named for Don Carlos Luis, pretender to the Spanish throne. The four boys were educated at Westminster school, as their father had been, and some of the children clearly spent some time in Russia. For example, Vitale's older brother, Charles, is described as winning the prize for Champion amateur sculler on the river Neva in St Petersburg and participating in steeplechases as a gentleman rider for Prince Soltykoff. He was presented by Tsar Alexander II with a cup for gallantry, before his untimely death in St Petersburg in 1863 at the age of twenty-four. Charles Eastland and Mary brought back ferns from their son's grave on leaving St Petersburg three years later. [154]

Vitale's childhood letters to his father and his sister Nina suggest an affectionate family, if somewhat dispersed. While Vitale is at preparatory school in Surbiton, he clearly misses his parents greatly. He writes a rather formal and restrained letter shortly after his tenth birthday,

'Dear Papa

I thank you very much for that half-crown which you gave me and thank Mama very much for the nice cake she gave me. Please tell Nina that I have not forgotten to send the paper which she asked me to send and I hope she will like it. And give the little book to [Carlotta] Louisa. I am quite well.

Ask Nina to write to me soon. May I take a play box.

Leopold has been to see me today.
Please believe me to be
Your affectionate son, Vitale Domenico de Michele, [155]

His subsequent letters are less formal -

Surbiton, April 2 1859 - 'I should like dear Mamma to
come to England very much'
April 22 1859 - 'What month do you think Mama will
come to England ? I long to see her again. '
May 21ˢᵗ 1859 - 'I have not heard from you for long time
but I hope I shall soon have a letter... Be so kind as to
write and tell me where I am to spend the holidays' [156]

Before he started at Westminster School, however, it appears
that Vitale was allowed a trip to see his parents in Russia.
June 1 1860 - 'Thank you for letting me come out to you. I
never expected to at all'
He seems less lonely at Westminster, where his brother
Leopold was also a pupil.

October 30 1861 - 'Dearest Governor ... I like Westminster
more and more very day'
Oct 13 1864 - 'Dearest Mater, ...I feel quite different
since I came to Westminster, It is such a jolly place. I like
it very much, all the fellows are very kind to me , there is
not a single bully in the school. ' [157]

Other letters describe visits to Cyril and a journey with
Louisa, but there is no mention of Isabel and little of Mary
(although these two were by now in their early twenties and
probably more distant from their youngest brother). Vitale's

most affectionate exchanges with his siblings seem to be with Nina, five years older than him and the two remained correspondents throughout their lives.

While Cyril became a naval officer and Leopold went into the law, Vitale seems from the beginning to have had a career in engineering in mind. When he left school at sixteen, he began an apprenticeship with Robert Stephenson & Sons, the locomotive engineers based in Newcastle upon Tyne.

One of the most interesting keepsakes kindly passed on to me by the inhabitants of Turks Hill in Higham (see page 180 below for the links between the two properties) is a note book which Vitale started in 1864 to record his time at the works. This records that Vitale worked as a 'premium apprentice 'for Stephenson & Sons, learning to produce valves and engine parts and then graduating on to building and testing locomotives and steam ship engines. The journal runs from July 1864 to October 1866, when Vitale transferred to the pattern shop, which he seems to have found less interesting or worthy of record. Apart from noting his six week holiday back at home (a premium apprentice indeed!), the journal records an incident when he and one other engineer were thrown from a moving locomotive which was driven into a bridge in Richmond '*which was too low for her*'. Fortunately, '*none were badly hurt, except the stoker who was scalded*'.

The periodical, '*Journal of the Institute of Mechanical Engineers*' noted that during this period in Newcastle, Vitale '*invented a form of reversing gear which has been largely used in locomotives and marine engines*'. A reference from Stephenson & Sons, written on 13 January 1869 stated

'Mr Vitale de Michele served an apprenticeship of four years in our works, commencing July 1864. After the completion of this term, he remained for four months in our marine office as a draftsman.

We entrusted him with the care of the Engine we sent to the Paris Exhibition in 1867 and were perfectly satisfied with his fulfilment of that duty. We can report in the most favourable terms of his diligence, trustworthiness and general good conduct while in our service' [158]

It is worth noting that when Vitale represented his firm at the Paris Exhibition, he was only nineteen. He looked set for a glittering career in locomotive engineering, even at this age, until an investment by his father prompted a major change in his career. This brought him into civil engineering and, more importantly for our purposes, to Kent.

Cement

On his return from St Petersburg in 1866, Charles Eastland de Michele had become a partner of Francis & Co, a firm of cement manufacturers based at Nine Elms in London. Francis & Co. were in the process of building new works at Cliffe Creek in Kent and therefore looking for capital to fund their expansion. Quite why Charles decided to invest in cement is unclear, but it was certainly a decision which had significant consequences for his son. In his history of the Cement Industry, A J Francis says that *'during 1868... Vitale... was brought down [to take charge of the works]'* [159]. Perhaps it was a desire to set Vitale up in a career that drove his father's involvement? After Charles became the senior partner at Francis & Co, Vitale was appointed as manager of the expanded works at Cliffe Creek, himself becoming a partner of the firm on 1 July 1871.

Certainly, Vitale threw himself into his new role with gusto; Francis goes on to describe how

> '*One of his earliest actions at Cliffe was to invent a form of cement testing machine and this achieved much popularity among manufacturers, engineers and contractors. He then tackled the various stages of cement manufacture with a view to improvement, inventing a washmill [to reduce the slurry to the right consistency]. He next patented an adaption of the Johnson chamber kiln which allowed for drying a greater quantity of slurry before burning, but using less time*' [160]

The works at Cliffe (sited in part of the present RSPB sanctuary of Cliffe Pools) had originally been established by Francis & Co in 1867. [161] These were one of many works established in Kent and they brought new prosperity to a number of areas along the Thames and Medway rivers. Cement works - including those at Cliffe - were sited where there were natural deposits of chalk (usually low cliff formations) and clay (often in the marsh areas), as both materials were needed for production. In addition, the riverside locations were good for transporting the finished product and wharves were built at the mouth of Cliffe Creek to supply the factory, supplemented by a short canal running inland. In the early 1870s, as the works were expanded, a tramway was added.

The factory originally consisted of nine bottle (shaped) kilns; by 1886, a further ten had been added. [162] The works had one 160 feet high chimney (designed by Vitale in 1878) and must have been a prominent feature in the flat landscape.[163] The workers were also provided for in this rather isolated location - a public house, rather awkwardly named '*The Nine Elms Old Factory Canal Tavern Brewery House*' (usually shortened to '*The Canal Tavern*') was also established, and (rather incongruously) Vitale acted as the licensee, in name at least, from 1872 to 1893.

Commuting from Weybridge to Cliffe was not a practical arrangement in the nineteenth century, and so sometime between 1871 and 1874, Vitale began renting Higham Hall, some seven miles from the works. In 1874 he is included in the list of Higham gentry recorded in Kelly's Directory and, reflecting his status as a professional gentleman with a wealthy family, Higham Hall is listed as one of the eight named houses in the Higham entry.

As a consequence of this shift in emphasis in his career, Vitale became an associate of the Institute of Civil Engineers on 1 December 1874, and set up a private practice as a civil engineer, based at Westminster Chambers, London in 1877.[164] (Vitale's interest in mechanical engineering endured, however, and he joined the Institute of Mechanical Engineers as well, on 25th June 1877.) As Francis explains,

> '*He carried out various projects in the Kent area and designed several cement works, including one for [competitors] at the Pottery, Cliffe.*' [165]

In 1881, Vitale applied for the post of Engineer to the Rochester Bridge Trust. On this occasion he was passed over in favour of a lesser qualified man, James Appleton, supervised by the eminent civil engineer, Sir Joseph Bazelgette. Two years later, the Bridge Wardens decided they did in fact need a more specialised adviser and began a period of commissioning consultancy work from Vitale, which lasted until 1896. This included the production of designs for replacing the swing bridge element of Rochester's cast iron Victorian Bridge. [166]

Charles and Vitale's links with Cliffe also had a significant impact upon Nina's life. In 1871 she married the Reverend Iorweth Grey Lloyd, son of the Reverend Henry Robert Lloyd, Rector of Cliffe at Hoo, Kent and Chaplain to Thomas Longley, Archbishop of Canterbury from 1862 to 1868. Iorweth's mother, Harriet, was a niece of Earl Grey, promoter of the Great Reform Act of 1832. Nina and Iorweth had five children, and later letters make it clear that many visits took place between the Lloyds (by then removed to Wales) and the de Micheles of Higham. A letter of 1872 from Charles Eastland de Michele complains that Nina spends Christmas with Iorweth's parents in Cliffe, rather than with him, illustrating that parent/in-law tussles are nothing new. [167]

By 1881, Vitale's household at Higham Hall composed himself and two servants, John and Fanny Buckland, and the Buckland's two small children (Violet, born in Cowden in 1879, and Percy, born at Higham Hall in 1881.) * John Buckland had formerly been a groom at Vitale's family home in Weybridge, and it is logical to assume that he accompanied Vitale to Higham as a manservant from the start. Fanny Buckland originated from Cowden, close to John's home town of Brighton, and they had married in service. In 1881, Fanny was working as the housekeeper, and John as the gardener,

---

* Percy was subsequently to be one of those soldiers so tragically killed in the last days of the First World War, dying at the age of 37, on 1 November 1918

and they must have provided a welcome family atmosphere for Vitale, by now aged thirty-two, but up to now, wholly focused on his career.

Marriage and a family

Perhaps the Bucklands' example persuaded Vitale to look up from his plans of machines and cement works: on 15 February 1882, Vitale married Beatrice Theodosia Lake at Folkestone, where her father had recently retired from Gravesend to live. The bride was described as '*radiant and charming but evidently somewhat agitated*' in the newspaper report of their wedding.

The Lakes were a substantial local family, owning land in and around Higham. Beatrice's father was described in his subsequent obituary as '*a most prosperous farmer*'. He died just a month after Vitale and Beatrice's wedding. For many years William Lake was the tenant of West Court farm, Chalk (where Beatrice was born in July 1855) and of large farms at Stoke and Allhallows on the Hoo peninsula. The Lakes took up residence in Gravesend and William became involved in town affairs, '*serving as Mayor from 1874 to 1876 and as Chief Magistrate.*'

Fig 12: Beatrice Lake

This print from the Illustrated London News, dated Saturday March 14th, 1874, shows an eighteen-year-old Beatrice presenting a posy to the Duchess of Edinburgh, during her father's period as Mayor.

Beatrice clearly had friends in London society as well, as this letter from the librettist W S Gilbert to a twenty-one-year old Beatrice, demonstrates:

> *'The Boltons*
> *19 Sept 1877*
> *My dear Bee*
> *Thank you, once and once again, for the socks which fit*

beautifully. I hardly know how to thank you. I am glad
you can't see me now, as my emotion is unmanning me.
Bless you for fostering my declining years.
When are we to see you ? Socks are much but they are not
everything. They do not compensate for your prolonged
absence. My wife sends her best love and so do I.
Always affectionately
from W S Gilbert' [168]

Although the letter has a degree of irony, there was an ongoing friendship between the two. Andrew Rootes & Sue Williams's book *'Higham in Old Photographs'* includes a photograph said to be W S Gilbert posing in the garden of Higham Hall (which comes from items given to the Higham WI archive by Beatrice's grand-daughter).[169] Interestingly, Crowther's biography of WS Gilbert explains that in 1878, Gilbert was playing Harlequin in *'The Forty Thieves'* and was rehearsing his moves at every available opportunity.

'His hours of obsessive practice stood him in good stead
in after years: he took great pride in twirling himself into
the standard Harlequin poses for the edification of women
and children.' [170]

The friendship between the families was clearly more than an acquaintanceship - Lady Lucy Gilbert, who died after Beatrice, sent flowers to Beatrice's funeral in the 1930s.

But this is to jump ahead. To return to 1882, and her marriage in that year, Beatrice was by then twenty-seven. After a honeymoon in France, she and Vitale set about fashioning Higham Hall into a suitably fitting residence for themselves.

This clearly took some time and it is not until the turn of the century that the de Micheles really appeared to make their mark in local society.

To begin with, their home was still rented, and although Thomas Whitebread had died in 1890, it was not until June 1897 that his Trustees decided to auction the Higham Hall estate. Vitale purchased both the house and the land the following October for £4,875, (around £400,000 today) with a further £3 and 2 shillings for a stock of wood on the estate. [171]

For the auction, the house was described as follows:

> *'Higham Hall*
> *Comprising [a] comfortable old fashioned residence of moderate size, fertile garden, 4 cottages, agricultural build-ings and very desirable holding of productive orchard, fruit plantation and market garden.*
> *House, Gardens, Stables, 3 Lodges, 2 yards, granary and 1 cottage, let to Vitale de Michele, on yearly tenancy at rental of £110 per year.'*

The Estate included six acres of 'nearby arable' and grazing rights on the common. [172]

Maps of the house and gardens in 1895 and 1898 show the garden planted with fruit trees and divided into quarters, with the entrance in Taylors Lane. By 1899, Vitale is included for the first time in the list of a dozen or so private residents in Higham in Kelly's directory, indicating that by this point he had achieved a certain amount of status in the village. Despite his success, however, it is evident that Vitale needed to borrow money for the purchase - later family papers refer to a mortgage of £3500 taken out against the property.[173]

Vitale and Beatrice's only child, Dorothy Mary Beatrice, had been born on 3 July 1884. Dorothy's birth certificate contains an odd formulation of the house's name, which Beatrice gave as *'The Hall, Higham'*. Whether this was a mistake, or Beatrice's preferred name for it, we do not know. Vitale's occupation is recorded as *'civil engineer'* on the certificate.

The 1891 census records their household as still relatively small, comprising Vitale, Beatrice and Dorothy (aged seven) and two servants - Caroline Nobbs and Mary Jarrett. (By this time the Bucklands having moved back to Sussex to set up their own independent household, eventually becoming grocers on a small scale.) By the 1901 census, Beatrice and Vitale's household had grown to encompass a German governess for seventeen-year-old Dorothy (Charlotte Medenwelde), a lady's maid (Ethel Londwell), a cook (Annie Higgins), and four other female servants.

From then on, Vitale's upward trajectory continued. On 23 June 1902, he was appointed as a magistrate in the western division of Kent and throughout this period he remains in the list of private residents recorded in Kelly's Directory. In the 1905 copy, Higham Hall reached its peak, described in Kelly's as 'a principal seat' in the entry for Higham.

With his other preoccupations, it is unlikely that Vitale ever took a direct role in manging the farm or orchards. Certainly, throughout the latter period of their residence, the de Micheles employed a bailiff, James Ironmonger, who lived in one of the cottages across the yard from the main house (now known as Higham Hall Cottages).

One interesting detail is that, during her childhood, Vitale and Beatrice had commissioned a portrait of Dorothy, from a local artist - Kate Perugini. Kate was famous in her own right as a portrait artist, particularly as a painter of children, but she was also the youngest daughter of Charles Dickens, and presumably it was this local connection that led to the evident friendship between Beatrice de Michele, and her daughter Dorothy, and Kate Perugini. In 1893, Kate Perugini exhibited the portrait of Dorothy de Michele (then aged nine) at the April exhibition of the Society of Lady Artists, in Maddox Street, London.

A letter written by Kate to Beatrice at the time refers to the work she was doing for the de Micheles

38A Victoria Road, Kensington
15 May
Dearest Beatrice
I have been too busy until today to write and thank you for the sweet little muff and will take the greatest care of it. I have not yet painted it - for I am obliged to work away at a perfectly frightful child - I would so much rather not be painting. Do you mind me keeping it a little ?
I showed my picture of Dorothy to Millais[*] the other day. He likes it so much, I am glad to tell you, and thinks she must be a sweet little thing, but Beatrice of course he looks upon it as a picture and does not know how very much prettier she is. I know it and would give much to have her once more before sending it to you - but cannot ask you to bring her for another fortnight, as I have more to do at present than I can get through
Yours
Kate Perugini [174]

---

[*]   John Everett Millais (1829-1896) one of the founders of the Pre-Raphaelite Brotherhood

Another letter records how glad she is that Beatrice and Mr Michele liked the portrait. Finally, the de Michele papers include a very sweet letter written by Kate to Dorothy several years later, (it is addressed to Dorothy in her married name),

'My dear Dorothy
There was once upon a time, a dear little girl, she was about seven years old, and she was like - well exactly like what you like to think her - black eyed and red cheeked or blue eyed and yellow hair - or 'fair as a lily and brown as a bull' just as you like. She was a good child and wise too for so young a girl, but of course she had what we all have, a teeny weeny bit of a temper; she didn't show it often however - sometimes if the day was hot and she was tired and told to do something she did not want to do - there out popped the Teeny Weeny - or perhaps if she was cold and her little nose was red and she wanted to sit over the fire and warm her toes instead of going to the table and doing her lessons, there again the Teeny Weeny would show itself, but it wasn't often and never for long that she allowed it to get the mastery over her, and she was always very sorry afterwards where it did.
Well one day - I remember it well for I was there and saw it, this dear little girl was rather put out - there was a tiresome lady, a friend of her mother's who wanted the little girl to do the thing she most hated doing - that is - to be very still and quiet - and the little girl got rather angry, the tears came into her eyes and the colour into her cheeks and she looked as though she was going to cry, but all of a sudden and just as the tiresome lady was beginning to

think that the little girl was in danger of losing the Teeny Weeny altogether - the dear little maid remembered how it would grieve her mother were she to be naughty - so she pressed her little lips together and although the tears were still in her eyes - she said to herself 'I will be good' and she kept her word and sat as still as a mouse for just as long as the tiresome lady wanted her.

That tiresome lady will never forget the little girl's goodness and she does not want the little girl to forget it either, so she sends the little girl a little heart and chain in remembrance of that day.

I hope dear Dorothy that you have had patience to read this letter and that you will wear the chain, for you see you are the dear little girl and I am the tiresome lady and I am also your very affectionate old friend
Kate Perugini
And I wish you a very Merry Christmas and a very Happy New Year! [175]

Perhaps most intriguing of all, although wholly unexplained, with those same letters lies a scrap of paper, bearing the hand-written message

'Births
On Tuesday the 29th instant in Doughty Street, Mrs Charles Dickens of a daughter' [176]

Kate Perugini was born Catherine Dickens on 29 October 1839, in Doughty Street - and it is very tempting to think that at some point, Kate gave a scrap of Dickens family memorabilia to Beatrice or to Dorothy as a keepsake in token of their friendship, and that this perhaps was Dickens' own draft for the announcement of the birth of his favourite daughter.

Career Success

During the mid-1880s, Vitale's father, Charles Eastland was clearly still involved in the Vauxhall and Cliffe works - his letters in May 1885 record details of Board meetings and business deals. In 1891 he made a gift of shares in the company to Nina's children, which perhaps presaged some winding down from his business life - letters of 1892 and 1894 to Nina describe his deafness and the monotony of his life, although other letters from 1894 mention that he still attends the weekly Board meetings in Vauxhall. [177]

Charles was evidently still a strong personality in the lives of his children - one letter to Nina admonishes her to buy a lampshade for her dining room table, despite the fact that Iorweth, her husband, does not like the idea. [178] Another letter to Nina admonishes her that *you must have been ill, or you would not have missed your customary weekly letter.* Charles comments more than once that he is disappointed not to see more of his grandchildren, and in welcoming news that Nina's daughter Eleanor has 'come out' into society, he adds that he *feel[s] sure that [she] will not allow the success that attended her entrance into society to lessen her attention to those home duties which after all are essential to ensure her future happiness.* [179]

Whatever the respective roles of Charles and Vitale in managing the company, it seems clear that the cement business was a successful one in the last decades of the nineteenth century. Charles refers to the *extraordinary demand for cement for abroad* and his hopes that his investment *so long and laboriously kept together*' will begin to pay dividends.[180] Certainly Vitale appeared to be gaining a comfortable income from the Cliffe Works. As well as his growing household, he and his family undertook regular trips to Europe, including to Venice, where he continued his efforts to find the link between the Victorian de Michele family and the twelfth-century de Michele Doge of Venice.

On Charles' death in February 1898, Vitale became the senior partner. Charles left effects of over £19,000 to his family. Vitale's mother died in August that same year. In correspondence with his sister Nina in December 1898, Vitale refers to sorting out trust and dividend issues, presumably relating to the family inheritance. [181]

Vitale's work with the Rochester Bridge Trust also continued during the 1890s. In 1896 he put significant time into dealing with damage caused when a Lighter crashed into one of bridge piers, being thanked by the Wardens later for the 'energy with which he had conducted and supervised the work'. In December 1897, he was appointed Bridge Engineer on a permanent basis. Although there is some evidence in the Trust's papers of sharp exchanges over the level of Vitale's fees, his contribution appears to have been appreciated, with the Court of Bridge Wardens recording '*their entire satisfaction with the way Mr de Michele carried out his duties during the 19 years he acted as adviser to the wardens*' when his service to them ended. [182]

Thus, by the turn of the century, the de Michele family owned their property and Vitale was a successful and locally prominent civil engineer. He was patron of the Cliffe Cricket Club and a district councillor for Cliffe (coming third in a list of twenty-one candidates), as well as being appointed engineer for the Higham and Hundred of Hoo Water Company, in Higham, and serving on the School Management Board. [183] He was a Parish Councillor in Higham alongside members of local families of longer standing - such as Charles Lake (Great Oakleigh Farm), Francis Latham (Gads Hill Place) and Herbert Cobb (Mockbeggar). A reading of the Parish Minutes sometimes suggests some tension between the older 'grandees' and the new man of business, but on the whole, Vitale seemed accepted and respected by the gentry and villagers alike. Higham now had a population of 1,642 people, with a working man's club, recreation ground and parish council and was much more like the village we know today.

With offices in Westminster, Vitale was also developing his consultancy business. In 1900, the Association of Portland Cement Manufacturers was set up, a conglomerate that was to dominate the industry for the next seventy years. Francis & Co were one of the founder members of APCM but Vitale did not join the APCM Board and it was perhaps at this point, at the age of fifty-two and after thirty-two years, that he retired from day to day management of Francis & Co and concentrated on his consultancy work. In 1902, for example, Vitale was appointed to the sub-committee set up by the Institute of Civil Engineers to develop a specification for Portland Cement. Francis & Co were taken over in 1900 by the British Portland Cement Company, and after the First World War, the Cliffe cement works began to decline and they were closed in 1920-1. [184]

Freed of some of his day to day management responsibilities, it seems to be at this point when Vitale and Beatrice turned their thoughts to further developing their home into a fitting residence. Their first actions appear to have been the addition of a dining room and study on the ground floor, together with an improved staircase, and a main bedroom with dressing room upstairs. Probably a bathroom was added at this time also - dedicated water closets became more common in the late Victorian period.

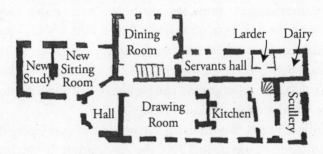

Ground Floor: Late Victorian Period

Fig 13a): the alterations made by Vitale de Michele

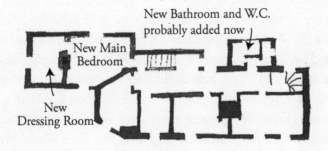

Fig 13b: First Floor additions, which gave the house a total of 10 bedrooms and 1 bathroom

These improvements cannot be dated precisely and may not have been done all at the same time. The dining room at least appears to have been done very quickly after they bought the house, as the outline of it appears on an Ordnance Survey map dating from 1898. If Vitale and Beatrice were unable to alter the house substantially before they owned it, it is interesting to contemplate how this aspiring family viewed the rather cramped accommodation of the ground floor before these additions (see figure 10a) on page 99 above). However, Vitale may have been allowed by Thomas Whitebread, or his estate, to extend the house earlier. The de Micheles also planted an avenue of chestnut trees linking Higham Hall with School Lane, perhaps with a view to shifting the entrance to the house away from Taylors Lane, where they may have considered the house to be a little too close to the road to provide a grand entrance. This avenue lasted until the 1950s, when Steadman Close was built, but these trees still grace the new cul de sac, even if the concept of a new, long driveway was never quite realised.

Further plans for expansion were drawn up, following the fortuitous presence in Higham of a Scots Arts and Crafts architect, Robert Weir Schultz (1860-1951), who produced a set of designs for another set or rooms to be added above the dining room. *

---

*   Robert Weir Schultz is also known as R S Weir - in 1914 he reversed his name to obscure his Germanic surname - in part to protect his wife, who was a local councillor

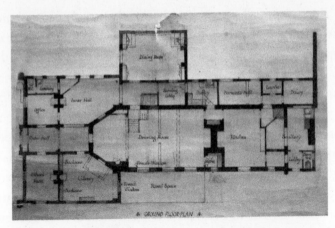

Fig 14a): Proposed alterations to the Ground Floor, which added a Library and School Room, altered the position of the front door and added a grander main staircase.

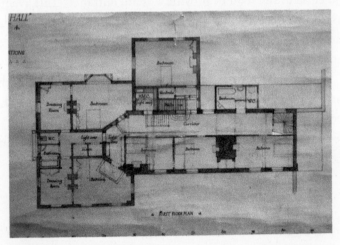

Fig 14b): Proposed changes to the First Floor, adding two more bedrooms, a second dressing room and additional bathroom

The second floor would have had a further bedroom. Although the total number of bedrooms would have remained at ten, the drawings envisage larger bedrooms, and a second top floor bedroom with a fireplace. This, and the plans for a school room, hint at provision for a live-in governess - which Dorothy had in 1901. However, it is difficult to date the plans - presumably they would not have been drawn up before Vitale owned the house (1897), and perhaps not before the death of his father made the expenditure possible (1898). There is also no evidence that the architect, R W Schultz was in Higham before 1899/1900. By this time, Dorothy would have been fifteen or sixteen but perhaps the de Micheles were looking to the future, and perhaps to any children Dorothy might have, as some of the planned additions seem a little late in the day for such a substantial investment. Or perhaps, as figure 14c) suggests, the plans simply reflected what Schultz envisaged that a substantial late Victorian home should contain - as befitting the de Michele's status.

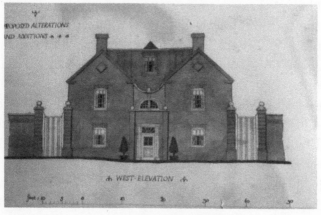

Fig 14c): shows the planned frontage on to Taylors Lane, which

would have been a significant change to the existing 'side on'
presentation of the house, and announce Higham Hall more
noticeably as a substantial house.

The appearance of R W Schultz in Higham deserves some further explanation, although it is not possible to tell in which order the following events occurred.

Among the de Michele's London friends were Lilias and Audrey Playfair, two unmarried daughters of the noted London obstetrician WS Playfair. Dr Playfair's son Nigel was a theatre director and known to WS Gilbert, as was Dr Playfair himself and it seems likely that the Playfairs or Gilberts introduced one another to Beatrice and Vitale at some point. From this link developed the Playfairs' link with Higham, and I am indebted here to the researches of the late David Barnes, one of the owners of Home Farm Cottage in Higham, who established that this house was originally built at the behest of the Playfair sisters, to provide country holidays for disadvantaged London children. [185]

Aptly named Holiday Cottage, the house was designed by Robert Weir Schultz, who was then working on some alterations to Dr Playfair's Hartley Witney property. [186] Vitale's involvement in the project is clear from his status as guarantor of the lease of the land (from St John's College) by the sisters. Completed in 1900, Holiday Cottage was overseen by Lilias and Audrey Playfair until 1921, when the creation of local social services made its role unnecessary.

Holiday Cottage brought Weir Schultz to Higham and perhaps also led to his work on Shorne Village Hall in 1904 and his commission to produce designs for extending Higham

Hall into a grander residence. Sadly, this planned expansion did not take place.

Death of Vitale

VITALE DE MICHELE

Fig 15: Vitale's obituary portrait from Grace's Guide to Engineers

Life seemed ideal - in 1905, plans were afoot for extending Higham Hall, and the de Michele's undertook a tour of Italy and Switzerland from mid December 1904 to April 1905. Vitale enjoyed travelling, writing to his sister in 1897 that travelling in any condition was more fun than life on an office stool.[187] However, in March 1906, Vitale was suddenly taken ill, developing meningitis. After a failed operation in Gravesend Hospital to relieve the pressure in his skull, he died at home on 21 March. The suddenness of his deterioration is described in the following extract from his obituary in a local paper

'On Tuesday, Mr Michele did not appear to be in his usual cheery and healthy spirits. He complained of neuralgia and a pain which he thought was caused by a gathering in his head. He remained indoors all day Tuesday and no alarm was experienced until early next morning when at 6 am Mrs Michele roused the servants. Later on Dr Pinchin of Gravesend was called for and still later came his son. At length it was deemed advisable to telegraph for a brain specialist and in due course Dr Lake arrived upon the scene. A somewhat serious operation was performed about 3 pm on Wednesday afternoon. But the patient never regained consciousness and passed away at half past ten at night from meningitis. [188]

It is ironic, but it is only at his death and from his obituaries that we begin to get a sense of who Vitale was. Thus in 'Engineering' (April 6 1906)

'In private life he was a congenial friend, one of the most loyal of associates and cheerful almost to optimism, while recognising difficulties he readily found means for overcoming them. He was an amusing raconteur and had a very wide circle of friends' [189]

And a letter to Beatrice from eight former employees at Francis & Co stated that *'Mr Michele was to us a good friend as well as a kind master and we are grieved to hear of his decease'* The Report of Vitale's funeral reads thus -

'The funeral of Vitale de Michele JP of Higham Hall whose death was announced in our last issue, took place quietly at Lower Higham on Saturday pm. Notwithstanding the

*inclement weather, a large number of gentlemen from all
parts of the district assembled in the church and at the
graveside and there was a goodly gathering of villagers,
the deceased being held in high esteem by rich and poor
alike. The service which was plain was conducted by the
Reverend Iorweth Lloyd, Prebendary.* [Vitale's brother
in law]

*The funeral cortege which consisted of a car and several
carriages left Higham Hall shortly before 3 o'clock and
as it passed through the village the greatest courtesy and
respect was shown*

*The remains were interred in a new grave and lowered
with the coffin were the floral tributes of the widow
and daughter of the gentleman.* * *The private mourners
[included] Leopold de Michele* [Vitale's brother], *Mr
Middleton* [Vitale's best man and colleague from his
time at Stephensons] *and among those present, the Mayor
of Rochester... Francis Latham, Charles Lake... Thomas
Aveling, William Stunt, Robert Arnold... Herbert Cobb
and sons... Edward Rosher... Dr Inman... J Ironmonger*
[Vitale's bailiff]

Apart from Mr Ironmonger, the mourners form a selection
of the 'great and good' of Higham and Rochester. [190]

Vitale's tombstone - which can still be seen in St Mary's
Churchyard, was designed in an elaborate Arts and Crafts
pattern by R W Schultz. Drawings in the family papers show the
original design with Vitale's half only having been completed.

---

*   In this period, it was common for the women of the family not to attend the funeral
     itself

Vitale's will left the fifty year old Beatrice an income of £200 per year (£15,000 today) together with the interest and dividends from capital and investments, in trust for her life. In the event of Beatrice's death or remarriage, his estate would pass to his child or children (Dorothy, in other words). His estate was valued at £12,137. Amusingly, an earlier version of his will, made in 1900 when Dorothy was fifteen, provided for her to succeed to the trust (in the event of her mother's death) at the age of twenty one; only a year later, Vitale had had second thoughts and decided that she should not benefit until the age of twenty five. One hopes it was not something that Dorothy had done!

A 1909 valuation values the house, garden and premises at £45 for rating purposes, and the farmstead (excluding the fields) at £37 10s. In today's money, this is a total of £6400. The mixed fields were valued at £3 10s, with arable land at £114 and the orchards and fruit plantations at £20. Altogether the estate comprised land at Gore Green Farm, White House Farm, and arable land along the Chalk road, as well as the orchards and fields surrounding the house. This came to a total value of £137 (over £10,000 today) and represented a tidy inheritance.[191] Beatrice would also have had shares in APCM, in all probability, resulting from the sale of Francis & Co. However, as was briefly described in Chapter 1, the first half of the twentieth century was one of increasing struggle for agricultural landowners, and Beatrice de Michele's subsequent experience proved to be no exception to this. It is perhaps fair to say that the heyday of Higham Hall, as the home of genteel society, was over almost as soon as it began.

Chapter 11

Beatrice, Dorothy and Adam and their children - the impact of two world wars on one family

The plans to alter Higham Hall were not pursued, and it is Vitale's untimely death that preserved the house in its current outward form. Vitale's death also forced Beatrice and Dorothy into the fore in our story and it is they who dominate the written records from this point on.

At the time of her father's death, Dorothy was twenty-one. A year earlier, her father described her as '*out visiting a lot*' but, apart from the fact that she accompanied her parents on their trips abroad and built friendships with her parents' friends, we know little about her.[192] There are occasional continuing letters in the family papers from Kate Perugini - these maintain a very affectionate tone - one of 1901 when Dorothy was sixteen says

> '*I am not ungrateful but have been ill [with rheuma-
> tism]... I am now getting better and want to see you.
> Could you and mother come to tea any day this week or
> next, or the week after?*
> *The necklace is the prettiest I have ever seen and gave me
> delight even when I was ill. I wear it as constantly that I
> fear I shall wear it out...*'[193]

One of Dorothy's activities as a young woman may have been playing golf at the recently opened Higham and Rochester Golf Club which had been created in 1891 on land at Oakland Farm (donated by one of Dorothy's Lake relatives). She certainly played later in life and it is possible that it was here (or perhaps some other local social occasion) that she met her future husband, Adam Brown Thorburn, a Lieutenant in the Argyle and Sutherland Highlanders. A battalion of the Highlanders was stationed in Chatham at this date and are known to have made use of the Golf Club in their leisure time. Officers such as Adam would also have attended local soirees, concerts and dance parties in and around Rochester society.

That Adam and Dorothy were acquainted even before Vitale's death is evident - Adam sent a wreath to Vitale's funeral, with sincere sympathy.

Born in October 1880 and thus five years older than Dorothy, Adam came from a prominent and wealthy Scottish family, the Thorburns of Peebles. They were bankers, mill-owners and tweed manufacturers. Adam's father Sir Michael Grieve Thorburn became the Lord Lieutenant of Peebleshire, Chairman of Peebles County Council and was a member of the Scottish International Rifle shooting team. Adam's mother, Isabella, was similarly prominent in local society, described as '*beloved in all parts of Peebleshire for her good and beneficent work*' (if the possible hyperbole in her later obituary is to be believed). She was also a breeder of prize-winning sheep. The Thorburns lived at Glenormiston House, Innerleithen, which had the notable peculiarity that Sir Michael held the freehold of his estate on condition that he gave the reigning Sovereign one red rose ' *when he (or she)* *passes that way.'* *

Adam was educated at Marlborough School and the Royal Military Academy, Sandhurst. He was commissioned a Second Lieutenant in the 1st Battalion Argyll & Sutherland Highlanders on 6 December 1899 and promoted to Lieutenant two years later. With his battalion he served in the Boer War, participating in operations in the Orange Free State, the Transvaal and Cape Colony from 1900 to 1902. Wounded in battle, Adam spent a period in hospital in South Africa, before returning home in the summer of 1902.

Dorothy and Adam were married on 30 July 1907, some fifteen months after the death of Vitale. A letter of 25 July written from Stirling Country Club from Adam to Dorothy shows that there were legal niceties to do with Dorothy's inheritance to sort out as part of the wedding arrangements. It reads

> *'This is the last letter from Stirling before I come down south. I will wire you what train I am coming down by unless you let me know when to come and then we will go straight to Rochester for the contract thing...'*

Less prosaically, Adam goes on to write

> *'Darling, it is good to be coming away tonight on my way to be married to the dearest little girl in the world. Oh sweetheart, I love and adore you.'* [194]

---

*   *Under a 'Reddendo' deal struck with the Crown in 1516, a token rent of three red roses must be made by [the owner of] Glenormiston House near Peebles, whenever the monarch is in Scotland... the deal may date from as far back as 1405, and... represents a symbolic feudal duty.*

Their wedding, five days later, was reported thus in the local press:

> **'Smart Local Wedding**
> **THORBURN - DE MICHELE**
> *Many of the elite of the locality were present at St Mary's Church Higham on Tuesday, the occasion of the wedding of Miss Dorothy Michele, only child of the late Vitale de Michele JP and Mrs de Michele of Higham Hall, to Mr Adam Brown Thorburn, Argyll & Sutherland Highlanders, eldest son of Mr Michael Grieve Thorburn of Glenormiston, Peebles. The Bishop of Rochester (Dr. J R Harmer) tied the nuptial knot and assisting at the service were Canon Lloyd, uncle of the bride and the Rev W Burrow, vicar of the parish.*
> *The bride was escorted up the churchyard by two Highlanders in full uniform. She was given away by her mother and was becomingly attired in a white chiffon dress with old Venetian point lace, a train of white satin, a wreath of real orange blossoms and a tulle veil. She also wore a diamond pendant, the gift of the bridegroom.*
> *The bridesmaids were gowned in pale blue striped chiffon, blue and lace hats with silver roses'*

Among the present list (which it was then customary to publish in the newspapers) were gifts from Mr and Mrs Nigel Playfair, Dr and Mrs Playfair, Miss Audrey Playfair, Mr and Mrs Perugini (an edition of Charles Dickens' works) and R W Schultz. Beatrice's gifts to her daughter included antique Russian turquoise ornaments, perhaps given previously to her by her father in law. After a reception at Higham Hall where the regimental band played (presumably in the garden), Dorothy and Adam left for a European honeymoon.

As his regiment was now back in barracks at Stirling Castle, the couple would move to Scotland on their return from honeymoon. Between 1908 and 1911, at least, Adam and Dorothy lived at 9 Clarendon Place, Stirling, a substantial three storey Edwardian villa convenient for the golf course and the Castle. 'Situations Vacant' advertisements show that Dorothy had a small staff of a cook and two maids, and in a later letter, she describes how 'all I wanted to do in Stirling was play golf...' (although this was not meant as a favourable comment on the course).

The marriage was also suitably celebrated in Scotland (although without the presence of the happy couple) -

> *Marriage festivities - last week Mr and Mrs Thorburn, Glenormiston, entertained the servants and other employees on the estate to supper on the occasion of the marriage of their eldest son, Captain Thorburn [sic], Argyle and Sutherland Highlanders, to Miss Dorothea [sic] de Michele, Higham, Kent. The supper was held in the servants' hall, which was nicely decorated with flowers etc. Mr Alexander, the overseer, occupied the chair. In a few appropriate remarks, the Chairman proposed the toast for the young couple, wishing them a long and prosperous life.'* [195]

It seems that from 1911 to 1920 Beatrice lived on her own at Higham Hall, with a small establishment of servants and with Mr Ironmonger managing the farm and estate for her. She is described in the census of 1911 as a widow and fruit farmer. (This indicates, by the way, that farming operations, particularly fruit production had continued at Higham Hall throughout Vitale's tenure; he was never recorded as a fruit farmer, however, as he had other, professional, occupations). Beatrice at this point shared the house with a companion, Nora McIntyre (aged twenty), Ellen Shepherd (cook, aged twenty), two housemaids and a parlour maid - all young women in their early twenties. In 1913, Kelly's listed Beatrice de Michele as a private resident and still described Higham Hall as a principal seat, although this status was lost by the 1915 version. In her early widowhood, Beatrice remained a leading lady in village life, hosting flower shows in her garden, serving on the School Board and riding out in her carriage around the local country-side. Her granddaughter later said of her

'If my mother and my grandmother went out for a drive in the afternoon - as they mostly did - they would trundle along in a carefully closed brougham lined with white and decorated with a bunch of sweet-smelling flowers' [196]

Mr Ironmonger, the bailiff, lived in one of the two Higham Hall Cottages which were then obviously still used for 'estate' staff. Despite the continuity of the village and estate arrangements, it must have been quite a change from the busy and sociable life the family had led before Vitale's death. That said there were frequent trips to Scotland and frequent visits from Dorothy. For example, Adam and Dorothy's first child - a son named Michael Vitale - was born on 10 May 1908, at their home in Clarendon Place, Stirling. Not only was Beatrice present at the birth, she also registered it for Dorothy on 26 May. Presumably Adam was busy with regimental duties as he was still pursuing his career in the Army and was promoted to

Captain the following year (1909).

The ongoing friendship between Kate Perugini and both mother and daughter is evident on Michael's birth, when Kate wrote to say

> *'Best love to dear Dorothy and a kiss. She will adore the baby very soon. An infant is a rather terrible possession just at first.'* [197]

which is a poignant remark when one knows of the distress Kate Perugini and her husband suffered at the loss of their own (and only) child at seven months.

The 1911 census records Dorothy at Higham Hall as a visitor, along with the infant Michael, and his nursemaid. And when Adam and Dorothy's second child was born on 25 August 1912 - Beatrice Isabella Dorothy Thorburn - Dorothy at least was back in Higham and the baby was born at Higham Hall, again with Beatrice in attendance. This time, Dorothy registered the birth.

The Great War

The records are mostly silent for this period, but we do know that during the War, Adam served on the Western Front. He was promoted to Brigade Major (in February 1915), and then to acting Lieutenant Colonel in September 1918. He was wounded (some sources suggest severely) at the Battle of Loos in September 1915. He appears at this point to have been serving with the 10th brigade of the Highlanders, who for two days of the battle were isolated in a network of trenches under heavy German bombardment, suffering from drifting chlorine gas, which was used by the British Army during their offensive. [198]

Although Adam returned briefly to active service with his battalion from June to July 1916, he does not ever appear to have been fully fit after this experience. As result, he was subsequently appointed to HQ based staff positions. Later references in the letters between Dorothy and her mother suggest that after the war, Adam continued to suffer from shell-shock (Dorothy refers to it as 'nerves') which may have explained his withdrawal from the Front.

There are no letters between Dorothy and her mother during the four years of the War, which suggests that Dorothy and her children may well have spent the bulk of that period in Higham - particularly while Adam was serving in Europe.

After the Armistice, Adam was posted to Cologne, as part of the British Army occupation of the Rhineland. Dorothy went with him, leaving seven-year-old Beatrice with her grandmother at Higham Hall. Michael (then eleven) appears to have spent at least some time with his parents, although it is likely that these were short trips during holidays from his Brighton prep school (Brunswick School) which he attended up until 1922. Extracts from Dorothy's letters to Beatrice suggest that both she and Michael were enjoying the whole experience of occupation -

> *'The people are very docile... it's a six month prison job if they are unpleasant to me !! We have been allotted billets and I am endeavouring to housekeep. Adam does the conqueror with much éclat. He'd made himself ill with excitement before we came...*
> *Cologne is lovely - lots of smells and lovely shops with very cheap things... Most lovely toys and heaps of amber - also*

*white, coral and ivory beads… Grapes are n't ripe but there
are lots of other fruit and I've found a lovely blue salvia
which you will love if I can fetch it along. The place reeks
with goats… Our men behave as if the Hun does not exist
and you never see one speak to one unless on business. Its'
all very entertaining…'*

*'We have now more or less settled in. We have a German
woman who cleans the rooms. Adam's servant - a most
excellent boy - does butler and another boy does cook.
Our food consists practically entirely of rations but Gray
(the servant) collects any extra things… Mike luckily had
diverse extra things and is quite happy. He goes down to the
transport lines every morning and rides a rather pleasant
mule… also he comes with us to dances and concerts for
the men - he makes friends with everyone and is getting
just a bit spoilt'* [199]

In 1920, Adam was posted to India, and shortly after,
Dorothy again followed him, travelling by boat via Gibraltar
and the Suez Canal. This time, both children remained in
Britain, dividing their time between their grandmother in
Higham, Adam's parents in Scotland and, in Michael's case,
Marlborough College, where he had followed his father as
a boarder.

Dorothy's letters and diaries demonstrate that she spent the
next couple of years alternately thanking and chastising Beatrice
for her care of the children. Money seems to have figured largely
in Dorothy's judgment of whether an action was sensible or
not and at times one feels a little sorry for Beatrice, managing
two children in probably rather straightened circumstances,

with a fairly constant stream of instruction from overseas. In December 1920, for example, Dorothy writes '...*[I am] disgusted you are not coming out here...*' before going on to say how easy it would be for her mother to travel, and then asking when her mother will be sending out the hair prescription she had asked for. [200]

At heart, Dorothy and Adam seemed determined that Beatrice should keep up the house at Higham and the estate from the best of motives, but as time goes on, Dorothy seems to lack any understanding of the financial and emotional struggle her mother might be having. While she recognises that her mother has little income, Dorothy constantly complains about the cost to herself and Adam of everything. In this letter written from on board ship (August 1920) Dorothy apologises for her 'snappy' mood on leaving, but reminds Beatrice to

> '*remember that Adam has told Milly* [Adam's younger brother, Michael Percy Thorburn] *that whatever happens you are not to have to give up Higham because you can't afford it so he is to help you out in every way. And don't think anyone will think you are doing it for yourself- it will be for me - Adam insists that I must always feel I've always got Higham to go to. But I won't have you worry yourself to death for that end - I'd rather have you than Higham and you must tell us if you feel in a hole.* ' [201]

Dorothy's letters in December and February are a case in point-

> '...*I got two letters from you last mail. How good of you to send me all that account - apparently I owe you £3 10s*

168

*which I will send when my monthly rolls up in March.
I am very worried because it seems to me you've been
spending such a lot for the children and still you had only
just enough.'*

*'...Ever so much love darling and tell me if you want the
extra £12 this quarter or if you'll see again what happens
- some things - I notice on looking again are sort of what
would be spread over two quarters - Beatrice's clothes
for instance'*

Both she and Adam seemed resistant to his father's efforts to
make them cut their coat according to their cloth.

*'...I've been so worried in case MG took it into his head to
write panic letters to you about money. He did it to Adam
and has worried him stiff for he fondly hoped his remarks
had cured the old stupid of thinking we can live on nothing. However, Adam is quite firm and says the money has
got to come from somewhere (MG says the shares may not
pay this year)... I expect its all a fuss because they want
the children and think that we are making life reasonable
for ourselves here...'* [202]

At the same time, a diary entry in January 1921 records how
Adam, having won a lot of money at the races, has bought a
pony on the strength of it.

Beatrice's governess also seems to have become a bone of
contention - Dorothy did not approve of her mother's first
choice, a Miss Marsden, and in time was proved right. She
preferred her mother's next choice, Miss Sabine, but in the end
began to wonder if school would not be better option.

'I am sorry that you have had to get rid of Miss Marsden because I hoped you would find her useful but I always thought (after seeing her) that she was much too old...'
... get someone good... and then dump her in the morning room and leave her alone. Then it does not matter if she bores you or not. Any woman who has the sort of brain who can quite cheerfully cope with a child year in year out would drive either you or me demented because they all have a silly sentimental cast if they are really good to the children and fond of them, or else they are placid and equally maddening...' (Dec 1920)
'there must be some school that Beatrice could go to... I want her to have a uniform (not scrappy) upbringing. This must be achievable for £100 a year, or I will have to find more, although... it seems rot that it can't be...' (Jan 1921)

Divided between apparent exasperation with and clear affection for her mother, she reminds her that

'I am worried to death at leaving you with all the worry of the children, besides being worried at leaving them too... So don't be an old idiot. You do seem to be giving those kids a lovely Christmas holidays. Mike's report was better but I thought you were going to have a governess with them for the holidays and that she was to coach him. However, that will be for next time perhaps. I think it's only fair that he should get a little help... Mr Thring wrote a very pleasant latter full of praise about Mike's acting...'
'I enclose you an awful list of things to do... I can't remember if you 've had time to send the grey ball [dress] since

*I wrote but I rather think you have… I said you would
send [Mrs Hyslop] a sale catalogue of 'Elegance'. I meant to
send you a cheque this mail for what I owe you but I am so
tired after careering about early this morning that I really
can't hunt my keys and cheque book. You see I shall have
to start dressing for this afternoon before long.' (Jan 1921)*

The rest of the letter contains a lengthy complaint about
Beatrice paying the gardener (Grimwood)'s expenses for escorting Michael down from Scotland.

The garden at Higham Hall does receive sporadic mentions
in Dorothy's letters - in one to her daughter Beatrice she talks
about sending her some Indian seeds to grow, in another she
criticises the amount of watering required to create an English
garden in India and the general hopelessness of Indian servants
looking after her new garden. In another, she comments that
there are no more mosquitos in India than 'we had at Higham'
(given the proximity of the Thames marshes and their suita-
bility for breeding mosquitos at the time, this is not much of
a recommendation in practice).

Dorothy appears to have been well supplied with fruit from
the garden at Higham for her journey out to India, mentioning
in her first letter that

*'I have only just finished the peaches and figs and the pears
are just getting ready.'*

In a letter sent from Gibralter she also commented

'Bought some figs, dried and tasteless compared to ours'

In terms of India and the Indians, Dorothy reflects the

opinions of many Englishwomen of her class and generation. After describing Bombay as

'perfectly beastly... like a mixture of Earl's Court and a Paris back street'

she comments on a visit to the railway station in Poona (where Adam was stationed)

'I hadn't been to the station since I arrived and I watched the crowds with great joy. Its so curious to see a train - quite an English looking train - come in and then for it to unload the most varied collection of uncivilised people. Men with next to no clothes - children with none at all - blind grandfathers with sons, daughters, babies, cooking pots, musical instruments and bedding complete, and all perfectly alive to the usual way of travelling by train. Every traveller has a roll of bedding in this country because the trains takes ages to go any distance and though there are sleeping berths, there is no bedding on them and perhaps its just as well!! When I left the station there were several families quite happily camped on the platform. Of course the smart young Indian is quite above that sort of thing so leaves the station and gives up his ticket with what he fondly hopes is quite the English manner, even if he is saved the expense of socks by wearing brown shoes that match his brown legs.'

While this sounds patronising to our ears, Dorothy was quite clear eyed about the influence of English colonialism in India, saying that she thought the original settlers kept Indians ill-educated and underdeveloped for the better sale of British goods, which has left India ill equipped to defend itself and develop its own industry, as a self-sufficient country. She excoriates the East India Company as (also)

> *'beastly because of the utter lack of honesty, sense or even thought out policy towards the Natives and even for themselves, it was 'lets grab all we can and the devil take the hindemost (sic) '*

In Poona, Dorothy fitted out their bungalow with Indian ornaments and fabrics,

> *'not because I admire them as things, but because they 'belong' - nothing can make a bungalow look English... though of course everyone howls at my saris and durries'*

She spent her time in the same way as most military wives - visiting 'regimental women', going to the club and to sewing, catching butterflies, and attending dinner parties - which she describes as deadly dull because the same people were always there. In 1920-21, India was in some turmoil, with Ghandi promoting the non-co-operation policy and increasing demonstrations. In her first couple of months, Dorothy comments

> *'I fancy a good deal of this Indian unrest business is exaggerated or else the authorities were afraid it might get very much worse. I am told most of the better class natives know too well which side their bread is buttered to worry with Mr Ghandi - that is the Hindoos . The Mahomedans have no use for him anyway but he and others keep reminding*

them of the Dyer thing at Armritsar* [and the fact that Britain fought against Turkey in the war]'

Commenting on Diwali she writes

'But oh! the noise . There's no peace and quiet about the East. Myself I believe that the reason they never get anything done is because they all talk and scream themselves tired and then haven't energy to carry out what they've done all the screaming over - also I believe they are like children - afraid of both science and the dark'

But lest we conclude from this that Dorothy was irremediably racist, it is worth noting her comments in letters home to her mother about two of the servants at Higham - first a reference to '[a] tiresome housemaid and her consumption…' and then this about her parents' long serving estate manager

'I'm so sorry Ironmonger is a worry. I am sure he has always been under the impression that the farm was run to employ him and to provide work for some of these ancient people'

Perhaps instead she was just rather a snob.

By February 1921, after just six months in India, Dorothy was beginning to comment on Adam's health - telling his mother that he had had another attack of 'nerves' prompted by a bout of malaria. She writes to Beatrice that

'Adam is better again - I told you that he had a slight go of nerves last week over a row there had been in the

---

* This is a reference to the Jallianwalla Bagh massacre in Armritsar in 1919, where British Troops opened fire on an unarmed crowd of Indian civilian, killing at least 400 and injuring over 1000

regiment, didn't I ? He went out to camp and it did him
lots of good…'

As early as March 1920, Adam had relinquished command of his battalion and his temporary rank of Lt Col. The following year Dorothy's letters explain he has two months leave, so they are going to Ootacamund to camp, shoot and fish. Ootacamund was a hill station and summer resort in Tamil Nadu, often used by the British Army for recuperation for soldiers. Dorothy describes Adam as looking tired and being 'very fretty'.

But this did not effect a cure, in March 1921 she writes from Ootacamund that

> *'this climate is making Adam very jumpy… so that I haven't much free time as I must always be ready to sympathise or do anything I am wanted to at a moment's notice…'*

Still there in May, Oota (as it was often called) was clearly not suiting Dorothy either. She explains that they had originally been intending to go to Kashmir for a break but

> *'You know one does get furious with people. We had arranged everything in our minds for Kashmir and then leave came a bit early for that and a silly juggins who knows this place well, literally worried Adam into coming here and never told him a thing about it not suiting some people… He says he has felt much more miserable than when his nerves were at their worst - and I'm now told that this is a vile place for nerves. I believe all Anglo-Indians are fools except a very few and that their great idea is to impress on all strangers with the superiority of India above*

all other places because they are really so ashamed of the
rotten hopeless dirty slack futile uncomfortable way they
have drifted into living.'

By the end of May 1921, Dorothy and Adam were back in
Poona but the novelty of India had completely worn off and
Adam's health cannot have been improved by worries over the
financial viability of his father's business. In June, Dorothy
writes that the Mill in Peebles had been shut down, so Adam
would have to retire from the Army later, although in practice, this was not to be possible. She sets out in this letter that
they are hoping to return from India in the spring of 1922.
A subsequent letter from Adam in September suggests that
this new plan is only to be a period of leave and that it may
itself be unaffordable (a journey from India to England costing
£300 per person, each way). In December 1921, Dorothy was
appointed to the Managing Committee of the Ladies Club.

However, there is then an urgent and undated letter, probably written very early in 1922 which says

'This is going to be a funny sort of letter again because I
am going to see you before long so its silly to write. We're
coming home as soon as ever we can get. Adam has had
quite enough of this country and has gone - as I've seen
heaps of other people go - down with fever - temperature -
three days a week - only with Adam his nerves have gone
about as badly as they did in France, so the only thing is
home at once...'

As a result of this apparent breakdown and sudden change
of plan, Adam and Dorothy sailed home on the Kaiser-i-Hind,

with ten cwt of luggage, including seven big boxes and a number of suitcases. They arrived at Tilbury in late February 1922, Beatrice having made arrangements for their mountain of luggage to be conveyed to Higham Hall. Their address on entry to England was given as Higham Hall, although Scotland was given as their intended place of residence.

Military records suggest that Adam never served again; from the time of his return from India he was on medical leave and from March 1923 he was put on half pay. Doubtless Beatrice appreciated his presence in Higham - the letter of September 1921 referred to above suggests that she had sought his advice about managing the estate - Adam had suggested by return that it might be an option to let the arable land out and probably some orchards, with reservations as to recovery, but at the same time offering some fixity of tenure to ensure the maximum rental income. Thus, from the time of his return, it seems likely that Adam at least assisted Beatrice to run the estate and, in all probability, increasingly took the lead in doing so.

Finally, in December 1923, a deed of family arrangement was drawn up to formalise this change of ownership. The whole of the Higham Hall estate, the land, the parts still subject to a mortgage obtained by Vitale, all the monies in trust and in hand, and all the stock on the estate, were turned over by Beatrice to a trust managed by her solicitor, in conjunction with Adam's two brothers, for the benefit of Adam and Dorothy. The deed records the sixty eight year old Beatrice's wish to stop running the estate and the fruit farming, and to turn the land and business over to her daughter and son in law, in return for an annuity of £300, and the use and enjoyment of the house, gardens and 'pleasure grounds' for the rest of her life.

Unfortunately, this sensible looking plan was doomed not to work out. The next recorded event in the history of Higham Hall was a tragic one, which led to the ultimate departure of the de Michele/Thorburn family from the house.

The complete (and dramatic) newspaper report is in Appendix 4, but on 22 March 1924, a fire broke out in the house in the early hours and was well established in one of the attic rooms by the time that the alarm was raised. Although no-one was hurt, the house was rendered uninhabitable as a result of the damage. The family (at that time Beatrice, Adam, Dorothy and twelve-year-old Beatrice - the last two suffering from measles) and their servants needed to move out.

Adam Thorburn estimated that the fire had caused £1000 worth of damage (approaching £48,000 in today's money) and the Thorburns lost furs, clothes, books, paintings and furniture from fire and water damage. Added to the distress of the episode (Dorothy and Beatrice were described as being 'severely upset by the catastrophe' - as one might imagine so, this being Beatrice's only home since her marriage over forty years before), the financial loss was significant. Adam and Dorothy may therefore have decided at this point to cut their losses, repair the house and move out for good. Certainly, Adam's next recorded action was to raise a mortgage of £3000 on the house, in January 1925, with more money being borrowed in 1927. By 1928, the house and farm had presumably been repaired sufficiently to allow them to be advertised for sale in both local and national newspapers.

The house itself was described as old fashioned in the advertisements, suggesting that little remodelling beyond repairing the water and fire damage had taken place. Perhaps as a result, it took some time to sell - as well as being a period of general economic recession, it was a time of great economic difficulty for farmers. During the First World War, agriculture had been heavily subsidised by the Government and as a result, the pay of farm workers and the profit of landowners had increased. When these subsidies were abruptly withdrawn in 1921, followed by the lifting of restrictions on Canadian wheat imports, agricultural wages fell rapidly. It became harder for farmers to find labour and to make a profit on their production, and land became a correspondingly less attractive investment.

Adam placed the advert, which was described in the Times of 25 January 1928 as being, by order of Lt Col A B Thorburn (late 91ˢᵗ Highlanders)

Kent
Higham near Rochester
In an elevated position commanding exceptional views over the River Thames
Within a few minutes walk of Higham station (Southern railway) from which London is reached in about 1 hour
Three and a half miles from Rochester and 5 miles form Gravesend
VALUABLE FREEHOLD OLD FASHIONED RESIDENTIAL PROPERTY
Known As
HIGHAM HALL
Nine bed and dressing rooms, three reception rooms
Lounge, hall, study etc
Together with
FARMERY comprising HOMESTEAD of BUILDINGS

THREE COTTAGES
PASTURE and ARABLE LAND. ORCHARDS
And FRUIT PLANTATIONS
The whole covering and area of about
74 ACRES
Vacant possessions at an early date
For sale by auction at the London Auction Mart
144 Queen Victoria Street EC4
On Monday 30 January 1928 at 2.30pm

A feature in the Chatham News said

'*The announcement of the forthcoming sale of Higham Hall has aroused considerable interest in the village, for the ancient house standing in quietude at the end of the long chestnut drive, has seemed possessed of a romantic air, reminiscent of bygone days, when the maypole graced its meadows, and fetes and flower shows brought the villagers to its doors.*' [203]

It is not clear where Beatrice, Dorothy and Adam were living at this time. Between 1924 and 1928 there are various references in the Electoral register to Beatrice, and to Adam and Dorothy, all three of them at Higham Hall in 1924-6 and then only Adam in 1927. Beatrice was listed as living at Turks Hill in 1927 and this reference reappears in 1930, together with a phone number 'Shorne 9' which is recorded with Adam and Dorothy at Higham Hall from 1927 to 1929.

What we do know is that the current house at Turks Hill was built by Beatrice de Michele and has sometimes been referred to as 'the Dower House' for Higham Hall. A deed of February 1930 refers to the house at Turks Hill 'which has recently been erected at [Beatrice de Michele's] own expense.' It was and is a much smaller house than Higham Hall and would have seemed cramped for any sizeable family living there after Higham Hall, particularly a family used to a retinue of servants. Nonetheless, from the time it was built until 1970, Beatrice, Dorothy and subsequently Dorothy's daughter Beatrice, lived in the house. It is not clear whether Adam ever lived there with them, however, on anything other than a temporary basis. His later years appear to have been spent in Scotland, where he divided his time between Dalrounach, a house in the small village of Kilchrennan, Argyllshire, and Bridge of Wells in Lerwick, in the Shetland Islands, where he frequently travelled for the fishing.

The Higham Hall estate was finally sold on 22 December 1929, to the Hon. Mrs Kathleen Gay, who lived there with her husband Colonel Cyril Gay until around 1939. Before their story is told, we ought to conclude the story of the de Michele and Thorburn families, and their lives in Turks Hill, in Scotland, and finally in Ireland.

Beatrice de Michele

Beatrice lived at Turks Hill from the time she moved in in the late 1920s to her death on 19 March 1933. She was seventy-eight when she died and one imagines the last ten years of her life had been very trying for her. Although both Beatrice and Dorothy (in due course) left significant amounts of money on their deaths, it may well have been the case that both women had a relatively small income from their capital, and little power or inclination to convert it to income. One neighbour recalls Beatrice having the principal rooms in the house while her servants slept in the kitchen - which suggests a degree of loyalty kept them with her, rather than good rates of pay or working conditions.

Beatrice may well have struggled to cope with these apparently very reduced circumstances and the break up (if that is what it was) of the marriage of her daughter. Following her death in 1933, her funeral was described as follows,

> *The late Mrs Beatrice Theodosia Michele*
> *The funeral of the late Mrs B T de Michele of Turks Hill, Higham, took place at St Mary's Church, Lower Higham, on Saturday. ...Mrs de Michele, who was the widow of the late Mr V de Michele of Messrs Francis and Co, passed away the previous Tuesday at the age of 78. That she was esteemed and respected by a wide and distinguished circle of friends was evidenced by the large number present at the service while many old servants who spent happy times with the late mistress at Higham Hall, also gathered to pay their last respects.*
> *Among those present at the funeral service were:*
> *Mrs Thorburn, daughter, ...Mr M V Thorburn, grandson; ...Mrs C Walker and Mr C Walker, representing Sir Michael and Lady Thorburn; ...Miss Playfair, Miss Audrey Playfair; ...Mr and Mrs R Weir (Schultz); Col CH Gay; ...Mr J Ironmonger (manager to the deceased lady and 37 and half years in her service), Miss H Norris (24 years);*
> *Flowers; ...Lady Gilbert, Florence Lady Darnley...*' [204]

Beatrice was buried beside Vitale at St Mary's Church, and

'her half' of their richly carved tombstone was completed. She left an estate worth £5,400 (£350,000) in trust to Dorothy.

Adam Brown Thorburn

Adam died some five months before Beatrice, in his sleep, on a voyage from Lerwick to Aberdeen on board the St Rognvald during the night of 8 November 1932. The Evening Telegraph (9 November) described how

> *[Colonel Thorburn] retired to bed and complained of pain. He had a cup of coffee and when the steward called later the Colonel was sitting up reading and stated that he was now feeling well. He asked to be called at 8 o'clock. He was found to have died when the steward tried to wake him in the morning. A doctor later certified the death to have been of natural causes*

Adam was buried on 12 November, with full military honours, in the family plot in Peebles Cemetery, but we have no information as to whether Dorothy, or indeed Michael (now aged twenty-four) or Beatrice (aged twenty) attended his funeral. Neither do we know whether Adam and Dorothy parted on good or unhappy terms when he moved north to Scotland and she moved into Turk's Hill, or whether this was simply felt to be the best arrangement, given Beatrice senior's age, and their new cramped quarters.

Adam's parents died after him - Michael in 1934 and Isabella in 1941; they were both aged eighty-two at the time. All three are commemorated on the main panel of the family monument in Peebles, together with Adam's baby sister Catherine. There is no mention of Adam's English family. Michael Grieve

Thorburn left an estate worth £106,000 (nearly £7 million pounds today) but it seems likely (given the circumstances in which they lived) that not a great proportion of that travelled south to Dorothy or her children.

Dorothy Mary Beatrice Thorburn (nee de Michele)

After the death of her husband and her mother, Dorothy appears to have thrown herself into village affairs in Higham. After Beatrice's death, she lived on for another twenty-four years at Turks Hill until her death on 4 May 1957. She served as a manager (governor) of the village school for several years, attending all of the school functions and as Captain of the Guides, and Vice President of the Royal British Legion (Women's Section). She was a founding member and President of Higham Women's Institute and remained a member and drama representative after her retirement. At the time of her death, at the age of seventy-three, she had chosen the cast for that year's play and agreed to produce it the following September.

The report of her funeral, again at St Mary's, reads how her funeral was attended by

> 'many friends, and representatives of the Women's Institute, staff of Gads Hill Place School, Parochial Church Council, British Legion (Women's Section) and managers of Higham County Primary School. Individual gifts of posies were sent collectively by the school, WI and Girl guides and there were also many other floral tributes.' [205]

And that

> '*Mrs Thorburn will long be remembered for her gracious personality and interest in the education and arts and crafts of village life. She was a keen gardener and beekeeper and had a great knowledge of horticulture.*
> *The news of her death was received with sincere regret by all who had known and worked with her.*'

None of Dorothy's Scottish relations by marriage appear to have attended her funeral. She left an estate of £23,861 (approximately £500,000) to Beatrice, together with a number of valuables such as 'a chest of silver in Peebles… a suitcase of jewellery and silver in the bank at Gravesend, and the portrait by Kate Perugini.'

Michael Vitale Thorburn

Fig 16: Michael Thorburn in 1925, aged seventeen

We left Michael at Marlborough College and while the exact course of his career is obscure, some events can be traced. He did not stay on for the Sixth Form - the current school archivist commenting that neither Michael nor his father appeared from their records to be very scholarly. It seems that from the age of nineteen (in 1927), Michael was living in Scotland at Glenormiston with his grandparents, and possibly sometimes with Adam - there are references in newspaper social columns to Michael attending various events with his Scottish relatives, and no corresponding traces in England. In 1929 (aged twenty-one) he joined the Royal Naval Volunteer Reserve as a Midshipman and there are then various references in local newspapers to his attendance at training courses, and a steady progress through the officer ranks.

In December 1934, Michael's engagement was announced in a number of Scottish newspapers (again, not apparently in English ones), and he is there described as the son of the late Lt Col Thorburn (Adam had died the previous year) and grandson of Sir Michael Thorburn. Michael's fiancé was Marguerite Helen Walker, of Llanishen, Glamorgan, and they were married at the parish church of Llanishen on 29 June 1935.

It is not clear whether Michael's mother or sister attended and their personal papers in the Bodleain (whilst not complete) contained no record of any kind of this event (or indeed of Michael at all after his schooldays). After their wedding, Michael and Marguerite (known as Peggy to her family), returned to Scotland to live (at a small house called Hyndlee in Peebles) and, again, references to social events make it appear that they took an active part in Thorburn family events and concerns. Whilst this might suggest a degree of separation between Michael and Dorothy, it may simply have been the outcome of their economic circumstances - on his marriage certificate, Michael is described as a tweed manufacturer and it may well have been that his Scottish relatives could offer him a place in the firm, whereas Dorothy, with her smaller income, could neither offer him financial support, or indeed, a home.

From the outbreak of war in 1939, there is more information on Michael. He became a Lieutenant Commander in August 1941, after being mentioned in dispatches

'For seamanship, resource and devotion to duty in rescuing survivors from a Merchantman which was being attacked by Enemy aircraft:'

The stricken ship, the Archangel, suffered a number of explosions, and survivors recall the injured being terribly burned. Michael's commanding officer records how

'...the coolness and efficiency of this officer ...was largely responsible for the successful transfer of large numbers of men including some sixty wounded from the disabled [ship]... lowering boats while the ship was being attacked by aircraft from time to time, organising disposal of the wounded, and finally taking charge on the upper deck while the ship was lying alongside the SS Archangel. He was a tower of strength.'

Other notes record him as

'...of a retiring, studious disposition, with sound views in general - of untidy appearance...'

On 1 January 1943, Michael was awarded the Distinguished Service Cross. During 1943, he commanded HMS Lewes on her voyage escorting a troop convey from Britain to the Middle East and then on to South Africa, where the ship was used as a target practice for training. Michael may have found his war experiences hard to deal with. In 1943, a note on his service record by Vice Admiral Tait, then in charge of the South Atlantic Station, dissented from the recommendation to promote Michael saying that

> *'Before going to hospital where he now awaits invaliding from the station, my impression was that this officer was drinking more than he should'*

From this point on, Michael's postings were shore based, and he also had frequent periods in hospital, apparently suffering from cirrhosis of the liver and associated serious complications. At some point, this appears to have become too much for his wife and she is subsequently recorded on his service record as having moved to Underberg, South Africa.

After spending Christmas 1945 in Higham, Michael died from internal haemorrhaging in Chatham Naval Hospital (now Medway Maritime) on 3 April 1946, aged thirty-seven. His sister Beatrice was with him when he died. Michael is buried in St Mary's churchyard, next to his grandparents, and his brave and costly war service is marked by his Commonwealth War Grave headstone.

Peggy subsequently remarried and for a while, ran a hotel in the province of Natal. A relative who knew her as Aunt Peggy described how there was something odd about her first marriage - it was never spoken of in the family.

Beatrice Isabella Dorothy Thorburn

Similarly, we have only scraps of evidence relating to Michael's sister, Beatrice, but what there is suggests she stayed in Higham until 1970. She was born there in 1912, appears not to have gone away to school, and from the time that Dorothy and Adam left for India, Beatrice (then aged eight) remained in Higham with her grandmother.

Beatrice lived in the village for over fifty years, with her only lengthy periods of absence being recorded during the Second World War, when she served in the Princess Royal's Volunteer Corps - otherwise known as the First Aid Nursing Yeomanry, or FANY. Beatrice joined the Corps on 7 April 1938, at the age of twenty-five, and she served in both the FANY and the ATS as a driver. She served in the South Eastern Area, and was involved in operations throughout the War. She obviously got a great deal out of her service - it is worth remembering that this would have been her first taste of independence from her mother and grandmother - and she returned on a voluntary basis after the War, remaining as an instructor and administrator, based at their London headquarters from 1948 to 1965.

During the war, Beatrice was in touch with Michael - a letter to Dorothy written from Margate in 1940 describes how she (Beatrice) had planned to see Mike on his birthday, but all leave had been cancelled so she was not able to go. [206]

A letter from Robert Weir Schultz, dated December 1936, shows that Dorothy and Beatrice had kept up their association with Vitale's architect, on a social rather than a business level -

'My dear Beatrice
I think it is high time you began learning something useful as well as ornamental. I am sending you this little book in the hope that this you will study it carefully and become proficient in the most necessary qualification, viz: that of 'feed the beast'. This is perhaps looking forward a bit but

one never knows.
Meanwhile, I hope you will have a very happy Christmas
yours affectionately,
Uncle Rabbie' [207]

The letter presumably refers to a cookery book but also alludes to Beatrice's needlework skills - she earned both income and plaudits for her embroidery skills, stitching embroidery on ecclesiastical robes and teaching at Gad's Hill school in Higham after the War. It was presumably for this post that Weir helped out with a reference in 1946 saying

'I have known Miss Beatrice Thorburn for many years and have followed her career with much interest.
I consider that she is thoroughly qualified, from her train-ing and craft experience, to teach embroidery, design and the practical application of same.
I am sure she would prove a capable instructress and be able to hold a class together and keep its members interested in their studies.'
signed
Robert W S Weir
Member of Advisory Council
Central School of Arts & Crafts [208]

Anecdotally, Beatrice was also fond of acting - she met Sybil Thorndike who was an old girl of Beatrice's school in Rochester (Rochester Girls Grammar). Like her mother and grandmother, Beatrice was involved in village affairs, including captaining the Brownies and Guides, but as she grew older, it appears that Beatrice became increasingly isolated. Although she was clearly friends with Pamela Inskip, the then owner of Higham Hall, through a shared love of art, others have described Beatrice as 'a funny old stick' with a garden full of empty bottles. From 1960 onwards, she did nothing to maintain Turk's Hill, and on its sale in 1970, the house still had the gold leaf dining room ceiling that her grandmother had had painted in the late 1920s (and which apparently mirrored the original ceiling in the dining room at Higham Hall).

There was considerable surprise among the people of Higham when Beatrice sold Turk's Hill in 1970 and moved to County Cork in Ireland to live in an isolated house near two of her friends - the landscape painter Alicia Boyle and the writer, Patricia Hutchins. Patricia Hutchins' family had lived in Gravesend in the nineteenth century (they moved to Wiltshire because they could not abide the pervasive smell of tar in Gravesend), and Alicia Boyle attended art college in London - she once referred scathingly to attending

> *'an art training college for lady teachers... a backwater... [where they]...wanted me to learn embroidery but I rebelled'*

While this should not have endeared her to Beatrice, all three were friends, although it is not at all clear when or how they met.

It seems that Beatrice (or the Trust set up in her name, at least) still owned a small amount of land in the area after the sale of Turk's Hill; probably the farmland next to Turk's Hill's garden which formed the remainder of the original large field where the house had been built. Evidence in the Strood Rural District Council Records suggest that the Trust attempted to make over land abutting Taylors Lane for development in 1971, but that planning permission for this was refused.

Before she left, Beatrice donated Kate Perugini's portrait of Dorothy de Michele to the Guildhall Museum in Rochester, so that it remains in the locality where both women grew up.[209] It is sometimes on show there and my research enabled Kate Perugini's biographer, Lucinda Hawskley to track it down, which was pleasing. I was told that Beatrice cut pieces out of other family pictures to take with her to Ireland, when they were too large to transport, and for a while I was very concerned lest the Perugini portrait had been similarly treated.

Beatrice remained in Ireland until her death in 1983. She left an estate of £85,473, most of which was bequeathed to Alicia Boyle, apart from a legacy of £1000 to St Mary's Church, Higham and a similar amount to the WTS (FANY's Transport Division).[210]

Turks Hill was sold to Judy and Malcolm McDonald, who very kindly provided me with a lot of the foregoing information. As a final postscript, when the McDonalds themselves moved from Turks Hill in 2014, after forty-four years, they handed several items over to me, including original title abstracts for their house, estate agents particulars from 1950 for Higham Hall, some of Beatrice's beautiful embroidery, Vitale's journal from his time at Stephenson's, his wooden travelling box, and Dorothy's trunk emblazoned with the initials DMBT. The latter we left in the loft at Higham Hall when we moved, and the other items we have passed on to museums and archives to be stored.

Chapter 12

Society women and army officers

Kathleen and Cyril Gay

In 1930, Higham Hall and most of it's surrounding farmland was sold to the Hon. Mrs Kathleen Gay. Kathleen, by then in her forties, was married to Lieutenant Colonel Cyril Gay, and the couple moved in to Higham Hall, occupying the house and running the farm for the next seven or eight years. The field around Turk's Hill no longer formed part of the estate, of course, and other parcels of land from the estate were probably sold off separately at this time - for example, the row of houses in Lower Chalk Road called Michele Cottages were built in the 1930s on a strip of land originally belonging to the Higham Hall estate. They were originally named just 'Council Houses' and renamed Michele Cottages in 1961.[211]

Kathleen Gay was born in June 1890, the eldest daughter of William Robson MP, who was successively Solicitor and Attorney General in Asquith's Government before the First World War. In 1910, Robson was made a Lord of Appeal, thus bestowing the style of Honourable on his children. Kathleen Robson grew up in London, with a privileged lifestyle - the 1901 census records the household as having eleven in-house servants. Kathleen followed a traditional society girlhood in some respects, earning regular mentions in the columns of '*The Tatler*' -she was the bridesmaid at well over half a dozen society weddings before her own marriage, for example. However, as her sister explained, there was much more to Kathleen than a life of privilege:

> '*all her life[she] gave up much of her time to doing voluntary social work. During World War I [then in her mid twenties] she worked for the Red Cross and during World War II for the Soldiers and Sailors Families' Association. She had a genius for friendship, particularly with the young, and her sympathy and understanding won the devotion of all her nephews and nieces and great nephews and nieces of all ages.*'[212]

A piece on Kathleen's engagement (see below) describes her (at the age of thirty-two) as

> '*...a very attractive girl. She has one brother... who greatly distinguished himself during the War, and two married sisters. As a family, they are very artistic, having inherited their taste from Lady Robson's family, who left the latter and her children many articles of virtu...*'[213]

The Dundee Courier appeared less impressed by Kathleen's social conscience than her physical and artistic qualities - and this is a useful indication of what was expected of a well-heeled young woman in the 1930s.

THE BRIDEGROOM GREETS ONE OF THE JUVENILE BRIDESMAIDS.
Photo 'Daily Mirror.'

Fig 17: the marriage of Kathleen Roberts and Cyril Gay in 1923

Cyril Gay was the son of a Wiltshire vicar. Born in 1884, he was six years older than Kathleen. After studying for a degree at Merton College, Oxford, he was commissioned into the Royal Artillery in 1905. Promoted to Captain in 1914, Cyril Gay served on the Western Front throughout the First World War, earning a DSO on 1 January 1918, alongside the Belgian order of Leopold and the Croix de Guerre. [214] He and Kathleen married in January 1923, in the Westminster church of St Margaret's. Cyril was then thirty-nine, and a Lieutenant Colonel, and Kathleen was thirty-three. Cyril is described in the report of their marriage as '*the gallant bridegroom, one of the youngest Colonels in the Army*'.[215] Again, Kathleen's most interesting feature was deemed to be her appearance, and her decision to wear green as a going away outfit,

> '*When travelling to the South of France for the honeymoon, the bride will wear dark green marocain, showing her utter disregard of superstition.*'[216]

Four years after their marriage, Cyril retired from the Army, and possibly from that point, the couple relied on Kathleen's money. They were certainly a reasonably wealthy couple - on her death in 1968, Kathleen left £40,000 - nearly half a million pounds in today's money.

One of Kathleen's particular interests was science - she was a Fellow of the Royal Society of Astronomers, and she later developed an interest in research into psychic phenomena. She tried to apply scientific methods when examining the claims of various mediums and exploring whether ESP was a genuine ability.

The Gays had no children and there is no information why they moved to Higham Hall and took up fruit farming - perhaps Cyril was looking for an occupation after his retirement from the Army. We have seen that fruit farming had achieved the status of a major industry in Kent by the early twentieth century, due to a rapid increase in national demand, and North Kent was favourably placed to take advantage of the London market. [217]. Both Cyril and Kathleen became involved in local affairs - both were school managers (today's school governors) and the following cutting from the Chatham News shows that Kathleen continued her unofficial social work in the area:

> *'Peer's Daughter Cleaned House*
> *The Hon. Mrs Kathleen Gay… gave evidence at Chatham, Monday, when a father of 13 children, was charged with neglecting three of them. She said that after the man's wife died she helped him to clean out the house and gave the children new clothes.*
> *Mrs Gay added that afterwards the house became neglected*

*again, and she arranged for the two babies to go to
an orphanage…'*

Despite their occupations, the Gays may nonetheless have
found the rural lifestyle too different from living in London -
Kathleen in particular had always lived there, and must have
found Higham very different from her former life in Eaton
Square. There is evidence that she made significant alterations
to the house -unfortunately the planning applications that were
made for this have been lost in the Medway Local Studies
Archive. My assumption is that it was Kathleen who changed
the dressing room into a bathroom for the main bedroom and
added a second floor bathroom as well as two downstairs toilets.
If this is the case, then the house now substantially reflects
Kathleen's changes in its layout.

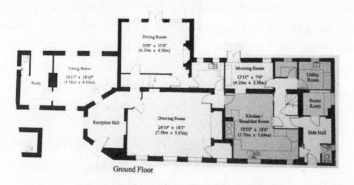

*Fig 18a): the house now - probably reflecting its
configuration in the 1930s*

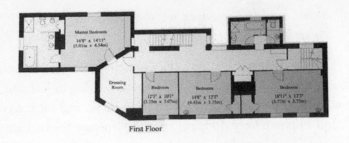

First Floor

*Fig 18b): the First Floor, with master ensuite and dressing
room, made out of the 'tower' bedroom. The one surviving
difference from this plan was the retention of the large
4th bedroom - made from the dressing room
and smallest bedroom combined.*

Having run the farm from 1930 to the late 1930s, the Gays
had survived the difficult period of wartime subsidy repeal, and
so the farm's profits should have been on an upward trend by
the time they left, in around 1937 or 1938. After their flirta-
tion with the countryside, the Gays returned to London and
remained there for the rest of their lives - Cyril died in 1949,
some twelve years later, while they were living in Chelsea, and
Kathleen then moved to Kensington, where she died nearly
twenty years later, in 1968.

To begin with, Kathleen retained ownership of Higham Hall
and rented the house and land to the next occupants - John
and Betty Lascelles. The Lascelles lived in Eaton Place before
moving to Higham, and it is conceivable that Kathleen Gay,
at least, had first come to know them because her mother was
still living in the Robson family home in Eaton Square.

John and Betty Lascelles

The Lascelles had no family connection with Higham - again it was work that brought them to North Kent. John Norman Pulteney Lascelles was born in 1899 to an Army family then living in the Curragh, Ireland. His father George was a Captain in the Royal Fusiliers, and John followed his father's profession, joining the Coldstream Guards in August 1917, at the age of nineteen. He was wounded soon afterwards, at the battle of Passchendaele. This battle was also the occasion of the death of Betty's father (see below).

We don't know how they met, but John and Betty became engaged in July 1931 - he was then thirty-two and Betty twenty-nine, so neither were in the first flush of youth. Betty came from a 'society' background - she had 'come out' in 1921, and frequently appeared on the pages of the Sketch and the Tatler during the mid 1920s - mostly attending hunts and hunt balls, often in the company of her mother, Lady Robert Manners.

Betty's father, Lord Robert Manners, was the fourth son of the 7th Duke of Rutland, a soldier who fought in the Boer War, gaining a DSO and CMG for gallant conduct. Robert was joint Master of the Belvoir Foxhounds from 1912 and one of the earliest society news reports of Betty is of her attending 'cubbing' (a sort of junior hunt) with her father at the age of eight. At the outbreak of War in 1914, Robert joined up again, fighting with the Northumberland Fusiliers for three years, until his death on 11th September, 1917 at Passchendaele. The Grantham Journal of 22nd September eulogised him as follows

'...we can have no hesitation in saying that the valiant Lord Robert Manners has gone to his rest full of glory and

honour, after worthily taking his share in the defence of
King and country. Typical of so many of high descent, he
possessed martial spirit in a very high degree...'

Betty was fourteen when her father died. For her mother, it was sadly a second bereavement - she had lost her first husband to wounds suffered during the Boer War.

At some point in the later 1920s, Betty left her hunting and socialising life and moved permanently to London. She began working in a Department store - whether this was because she had not 'secured a husband' in her first few years in society and needed to supplement her income, or whether she just wanted to become independent, is not clear. Either way it was a fairly unusual step for a young lady of her background, and was mentioned as being of interest in the subsequent newspaper accounts of her engagement and marriage a few years later. Having become engaged Betty left her job and she and John Lascelles were married from the Duke of Rutland's house in January 1932. The many descriptions of their wedding in the newspapers describe her aristocratic background and her husband's military career.

For example, in the Yorkshire Post of January 25th, 1932

'Captain John Lascelles and Miss Betty Manners, who
are to be married at the Guards chapel today, will begin
their married life well equipped with silver and glass...
among the most useful is the coffee making apparatus
which Princess Alice and the Earl of Athlone have chosen
as a gift to Captain Lascelles whom they knew so well when
he was on the Governor General's staff in South Africa,
and her friends of the Belvoir Hunt have clubbed together

to give the bride a diamond wrist watch… The Duke of Rutland, who is her cousin and will give away the bride, has joined with the Duchess in the gift of a topaz and diamond pendant…'

and in the Sheffield Telegraph:

'She made a wonderfully picturesque figure in her long clinging dress of plain gold tissue. The exceptionally long train fell from her shoulders like a stream of gold and a fairy-like headdress of orange blossom, arranged like a starry halo, held the exquisite net and Limerick lace veil lent by her cousin, Lady Violet Benson. Lady Violet, who is a sister of the Duke of Rutland, had also lent the massive diamond cross which glittered on the corsage, swinging from a string of pearls. '

The striking head-dress worn by Miss Betty Manners at her wedding to Captain John Lascelles in the Guards' Chapel, Wellington Barracks.

Fig 19: Betty Manners (Elizabeth Lascelles) on her wedding day in 1932

To begin with, the couple lived in London; Betty's mother was staying with them at their Eaton Place home when she died in January 1934, and the couple's son, Rupert, was born in Chelsea in March 1935. As part of John's military training, however, he had to spend some time at the senior officers' school in Sheerness, on the Isle of Sheppey. During this period, John and Betty rented Higham Hall, and the associated fruit farm, from Kathleen Gay. They enjoyed living there so much that they then made arrangements to buy the house and land from her - although it quickly became clear that this transaction took place at a very difficult time in the Lascelles' lives.

A lovely day at Lingfield. Capt. and Mrs. John Lascelles enjoy the racing to the full

Fig 20: John and Betty Lascelles

To begin with, John's father George died in February 1939. At the time, George was seventy-five years old, and John was forty-one, but George's death seems to have affected John very badly. How much of this was emotional distress is not clear, but it certainly affected his physical health. A local newspaper subsequently commented

> *'Lieutenant-Colonel John Lascelles had not been well since the death of his father several months ago. He spent a considerable time at Ashley* [his mother and father's home] *and later went to a nursing home in London'* [218]

And although the purchase of Higham Hall from Kathleen was completed on 29 September 1939, very sadly, John died at Higham, some two weeks later on 11 October. The cause of his death was infective endocarditis and sepsis - in other words some catastrophic infection, which as a rapid onset condition, is rather at odds with the foregoing comments, unless John had been suffering for some months from a low-grade infection which reached a crisis in the autumn. The date of his death was also the first day that the British Army saw action in the Second World War, with John's Coldstream Guards fighting with the British Expeditionary Force. As a serving soldier in a time of hostilities, John has a Commonwealth War grave headstone in St Mary's Churchyard where he lies - this has led some local researchers to assume he was killed in very early action in France, but the truth is more prosaic.

The announcement of his death reads

> *'After having arrived to take up residence at Higham Hall only a few days previously, the death occurred on*

Wednesday of Lieutenant-Colonel John Norman Pulteney
Lascelles of the Coldstream Guards… He served in the last
War and was wounded'

One can only feel for Betty, left with a four-year-old son, and no longer able to share the family home with the man she loved. Although she moved from Higham Hall after the war, she was buried in Higham beside John on her death in 1986, some forty years after she left the village.

There were practical issues to sort out because John had not left a will. Probate was only granted under letters of administration six months later, to Betty and to John's brother-in-law, Edward Seymour. John Lascelles left £8,341 (£330,000 today) and a trust was set up to own and manage the estate in conjunction with Betty. The Trustees were Guy Holford Benson, a member of the banking family, Kleinwort Benson, who had married a cousin of Betty's (Lady Barbara Violet Manners, daughter of the Duke of Rutland), and Colonel John Bevan, who served as an intelligence officer in the Army and subsequently became a stockbroker. Given the central role that Bevan played in intelligence operations during the War, it seems highly likely that in practice he was unable to provide much support to Betty - but, on the other hand, from her son's descriptions of her, I am not sure that she needed a great deal of help and probably the trustees were content to let her get on with running the estate.

A December 1941 survey of the estate describes it as having

> *'A' class management, good land and pasture, adequate*
> *fertiliser use…'*

and comments that

> '[the] Farm is greatly improved from last year and is carry-
> ing an excellent crop of wheat on newly ploughed pasture'

which gives the impression that Betty was learning her new
role very quickly.[219]

The survey describes the farm as growing raspberries, black-
currants, redcurrants, white currants, and gooseberries - in
total, five acres of soft fruit. Few vegetables were grown (mostly
fodder crops), and there were twenty acres of wheat, six acres of
oats, and six of rye, one acre of potatoes, five of mangolds, one
and half acres of kale and one of cabbage, and with forty-eight
acres of orchards. Five men were employed full time, along with
a further five casual and seasonal workers. The farmyard was
well stocked with animals - two cows, eight pigs, eighteen geese
and thirty-six chickens, along with one horse for farm work.
The survey does not say whether Betty had a horse to ride, but
does note that there were no tractors for ploughing (perhaps
not surprising on a predominantly fruit growing farm). The
total acreage was seventy-eight acres, which is remarkably similar to the historic size of the estate.

As for the house, the survey notes that the house and buildings both had piped water and electricity - presumably a result
of Kathleen Gay's alterations. It is described as a six bedroomed
old brick and tile residence with a lounge and reception rooms,
a servants' hall, kitchen, scullery, dairy, pantry and two laun-
dries. One odd reference is to a conservatory, which I cannot
easily place. The description mentions lighted lamps in the
walled garden, and lawn water (irrigation) laid on. The three
brick cottages are described as being let to servants, although

this may include the farmworkers. The outbuildings are listed as a stable, barn and cow loft, malt house, fruit store and (another) laundry, granary and cart loft.[220]

In March 2012, I spoke to the late Rupert Lascelles, John and Betty's son about his recollections of living there. Having moved to Higham Hall aged about two, Rupert lived there until he was eleven, and he remembered it as an exciting place to grow up, particularly the long tree lined drive which was such a good place to find chestnuts (conkers). The tunnel story resurfaced in his time - he told me how there was supposed to be a tunnel from the house to the farm buildings, but that he never found it. At the time the well was not in use and the main entrance to the house and farm were from Taylor's Lane. The tree lined drive was used more as a track and a short cut to the village - which may well have rather disappointed Dorothy from her viewpoint in Turk's Hill.

Rupert confirmed that Betty continued to run the fruit farm throughout the war. The apple orchards were mainly planted with Coxes Orange Pippins by then and Rupert described how, during the harvest, one woman was employed to polish each apple and wrap it in tissue, printed with Higham Hall Farm, before the apples were boxed up and sent to market by train.

The land at this point (he estimated) extended to around ninety acres, with Victoria Plums and cherries grown alongside the apples. As the men were away fighting, local women would be employed during the picking season; Rupert described groups of women coming from Chatham on the bus, bringing their babies in prams along with them.

Since Rupert lived in the house during the War, his memories are dominated by it - the dog fights in the skies overhead, incendiary bombs dropping in the village, and rockets twanging the strings of the barrage balloons installed by the RAF. He described his mother as somewhat eccentric, tearing around the village in her car dousing fallen incendiary bombs with sand. On one memorable day, Betty looked out from her sitting room window (in the west end of the house) to see a buzz bomb brushing the top of a nearby elm tree. At first, she was afraid it would drop on the house but it carried on to the village, where it fell on a house in Walmer Avenue, killing George Duly and seriously injuring his wife Alice. [221]

Another time a bomb fell in 'Donkey bank', directly across the lane from the house. The origin of this sandy mound and its name are both unclear, but it certainly served a purpose on that day as the bomb buried itself in the bank without exploding and was later safely defused. Wartime compensation records show that Higham Hall did suffer some bomb damage during the war, but precise details are not recorded.

At the end of the war, Rupert explained that the shortage of usable housing led to the compulsory purchase by the Council of land south of the end of the old drive - part of the field fronting School Lane was lost, and although the tree lined drive to the Village would remain (and still does in Steadman Close), it would no longer belong to the house. In the short term, prefabs were put in place and the longer-term plan was to build two or three small roads of houses on the land. Betty disliked the potential intrusion on her space - she would be able to see the new houses from Higham Hall (albeit only from the attics) and resented the nature of the compulsory 'purchase' - it is worth remembering that no money was paid by the Government for land taken under this scheme.

As a result, Betty decided to move, buying a more isolated farmhouse in the Sittingbourne area. This was Saywell House Farm, near Bedmonton, which may have been attractive because of the extensive stabling it possessed, and its proximity to the East Kent Hunt, which given that she was still only her early forties, may still have been an interest of hers. Saywell Farm is a similar type of house - a seventeenth-century construction with a large inglenook. Rupert explained that after moving to Bedmonton, Betty became increasingly reclusive, and certainly nothing further is known of her in written sources, until her death in 1986.

Higham Hall was not sold immediately and the timing of Betty's move is not recorded - she remained on the electoral register for the house in 1945, with no other adult resident. From some point in 1945/6 it appears that Betty rented Higham Hall out to a friend of hers (and members of his family). This was Ralph Pallett and his wife Doris and his brother, Douglas Pallett and his wife, Alice. One source describes Ralph as a farm manager and Douglas as a farmer, so it may have been that they worked for Betty and helped her to run the estate - although Rupert could not remember them having that role. It is not obvious how they would have met otherwise - both couples came from the Surrey area, and whilst Ralph at least served in both World Wars (in the East Surrey Regiment), their father was a commercial traveller in leather goods. As a family, they seem to have nothing in common with the Lascelles or the Manners families - or with farming, for that matter. Their relationship must have been close however - as well as renting Higham Hall for a period, Rupert recalls that when she sold Higham Hall, Betty bought a house on Romney Marsh for one of the brothers to retire to.

However they came to live in Higham Hall, the two couples divided the house into separate dwellings and lived there for around the next five years - from around 1945 to 1950. An estate agent's brochure describes the split as an *'Eastern part'* and a *'Western part... both self contained'.* The brochure also contains some asserted history - which does not accord with my researches in the least, but which could easily have developed as local traditions. For example, the house was described as being

> *'...associated with and probably used as the Toll House of the now demolished Higham Abbey that stood about a mile distant... the high walled forecourt was probably used as rest and night lock-up for Caravans and other vehicles waiting for the state of the tide to allow their passage across the distant ford... the fine medieval tithe barn... suggest that the Tolls, where payable in kind, were housed therein...'*

Leaving aside the fact that the crossing was a ferry and not a ford, the likelihood (as we have seen) is that the barn and the yard were simply farm buildings, built in a traditional way to support efficient management of the farmland. The heyday of the ferry, indeed, was some 200 years before the barn and garden walls were built - but we are used to estate agents making the most of the appeal of properties, and perhaps this is just another example of that.

Although it is not easy to visualise, the division of the house may have looked like this -

Fig 21a): the larger, Eastern section of Higham Hall

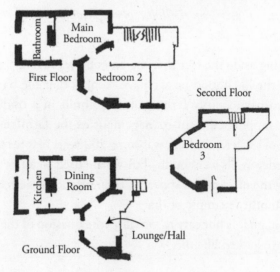

Fig 21b): the smaller, Western section of Higham Hall

The split was clearly quite uneven, but took advantage of the location of the two staircases. Although the circumstances of the Pallet's occupation of the house were perhaps untypical, this does demonstrate that after the Second World War it became increasingly difficult for a comparatively small farm to 'support' or even justify, a large residence at its centre. And when Higham Hall was finally sold by Betty in 1950, this was demonstrated by the absence of any buyer for the house and farm as a unified whole.

As we have seen, after her death in 1986, Betty returned to Higham and was buried in St Mary's Churchyard beside her husband. The best memorial to this couple who seem to have been cheated of a happy family life is the walnut tree planted in the front garden. Planted by them, from a nut brought from Ashley Court (John's parents' home), the tree has flourished for over eighty years. Surrounded by naturalised bulbs in the spring, it is one of the gardens most beautiful features.

Fig 22a): The Lascelles' Walnut tree, planted in 1939

Fig 22b): spring bulbs

Chapter 13

Post-war fortunes and the division of the estate

In 1950, a very significant change happened to Higham Hall in that it became separated from the farmland that had been the reason for its construction. Betty Lascelles' sale of the house and land may have begun as an attempt to sell the whole estate, but it must soon have become clear that the days of wealthy middle-class farming novices - like the de Micheles, Gays and the Lascelles themselves - had gone. The farm would now need to be run as part of a larger, more commercial operation, and the house was too big and too expensive to run to be used as an efficient farmhouse. In some ways it reverted back to a previous incarnation, being used a comfortable family home offering an escape from life in London - only, this time, without land and an income attached.

The estate from here on has two stories. But despite the greater wealth of data available as we near the present day, these stories can only be summarised. Many of the participants are still living, and some working, in the area, and it would not be fair or reasonable to make the kind of disclosures or assumptions that the passage of time allows us to make about historical figures.

The original advertisements for the property in October and November 1949 list the property as one whole thus :

'The well known Residential Fruit Farm
Higham Hall
With attractive residence, thoroughly modernised with all services, in excellent order: 5 reception rooms, 8 bedrooms and 3 bathrooms, (the whole temporarily divided into two self contained dwellings).
55 acres of fruit bearing mixed fruit plantation and 20 acres of arable and pasture, 2 cottages and good buildings Total area 75 acres' [222]

However, on 30 January 1950, Roy and Sybil Batchelor bought the seventy-four or so acres of farmland and the barns and yards of the Higham Hall estate, without the house, for £8000 (£249,000 today).

Higham Hall Farm

Roy Batchelor, born in 1916, came from a local farming family who have long owned farmland around Higham and on the Hoo Peninisula. He had married Sybil Jordan (then twenty-three) in Chatham during the war (in 1941) and they had two sons, Guy and Max. Max Batchelor (who still lives in Higham) explained that his mother wanted to buy the house as well for a further £6000 (£190,000), but that was too expensive, and so they built a new house, Higham Hall Farmhouse, on some of the farmland, further up the hill and fronting Taylors Lane. Planning permission was obtained in 1950 and the family moved in sometime during 1952.

This 'new' house lies between Turks Hill and Higham Hall

and commands a lovely view across to the Thames. Before this, the Batchelors lived in the Red House, Kings Farm, Shorne. Max said that building a house was very difficult in the post war period because of the shortage of materials, so his father employed considerable ingenuity in buying materials for agricultural purposes, which then found their way into the fabric of the new farmhouse. In 1954 a large packing shed was also built behind the barns - it was nearly responsible for the death of Max Batchelor and a farmworker in 1991, when it collapsed in a gale with both of them inside. It was replaced by the newer (and hopefully stronger) barn that is there today.

Max described that during the 1950s the farm grew apples, plums and cherries, with the orchards bordering Taylors Lane all the way up to the village - which must have been a spectacular sight in the spring. Once imported fruit became cheaper, however, this was not economic, particularly given the age of some of the orchards, and the trees were grubbed up and crops such as wheat, barley, rape and peas (for animal feed) were introduced.

Roy remained at Higham Hall Farmhouse, farming the surrounding land, until his death in July 1976. He was survived by Sybil for a further twenty-four years, at least nine of which she spent at Higham Hall Farmhouse, and they are buried together in St Mary's Churchyard, as so many of the people from this history have been.

The farmhouse is no longer occupied by the Batchelors - their eldest son Guy lived in a house in School Lane from his marriage in the late 1960s - and Higham Hall Farmhouse sold in July 2007 for £1,050,000 to a family named Latter (although I do not think that there is any connection to the Victorian

Higham family of the same name).

Guy inherited the farm and farms it today with his son, Mark. In 2012 the farm was described as growing broccoli, cabbage, pumpkin, squash and artichokes. For a while, in the late 1990s, Mark Batchelor lived in one of the Higham Hall Cottages, which is still owned by the Batchelor family, with his girlfriend and now wife, Verity.

In 1988, the Batchelors sold the farm buildings which used to be a part of the Higham Hall estate - the barn, cottages and the range of open barns on the south side of the yard. These were converted to homes - see page 225 below.

Higham Hall

From 1950 onwards, Higham Hall comprised the house, and gardens, with the farm yard closed off by a gate in the wall, as both yard and buildings now belonged to the Batchelors. The deeds describe the boundary as

> *'two lengths of wall joined by a gate and partly used to support a cow shed and other buildings.'*

From seventy-four acres in the nineteenth century, the house now sat in one acre, and although various old fruit trees remained dotted around the gardens for several years afterwards, the link between the house and fruit farm was severed for good.

Higham Hall was sold to John and Margaret Porter in February 1950. John Porter was an estate agent and auctioneer based in Gravesend. He later became a prominent member of the North Kent establishment, appointed as a Justice of the peace in 1952, and subsequently Chairman of the Gravesend

Bench. [223] His obituary in the East Kent Freemasons news-letter listed the following - Chairman of the Kent Branch of the Royal Institution of Chartered Surveyors, Chairman of the Anglia Building Society, Chairman of the Hastings and Thanet Building Society, Chairman of the Gravesend Conservative Association, President of Kent County Cricket Club and a Deputy Lieutenant of Kent. He was also a prominent Freemason.

In 1954, after only four years, John and Margaret Porter sold the house to James and Pamela Inskip. The Porters moved with their two young daughters to Leaders, a large house in Hodsell Street, Meopham, where they lived for nearly thirty years - which suggests that this suited them better than Higham Hall.

James and Pamela Inskip

In 1954, Higham Hall was bought by Mr and Mrs Inskip - James Sandys Ker Inskip and Pamela Mason, his wife. It is clear from some of Beatrice Thorburn's papers that she established a strong friendship with Pamela, possibly over a shared love of art. However, it must have been strange for her to visit Pamela, now living in her own childhood home - and even more for Dorothy if she also visited.

Born in February 1901 in Leyton (Essex), James Inskip and his three sisters came from a firmly upper middle class background - their father was Suffragen Bishop of Barking and his Uncle Thomas was Defence Minister under Neville Chamberlain and Lord Chancellor (as Viscount Caldecote) in Churchill's wartime government. James studied engineering at Cambridge University and then began working at ES & A Robinson, a printing and stationery firm in Bristol which made important advances in the development of mass production techniques. His interest appears to have been in aeronautical engineering. President of the Cambridge University Aeronautical Society, James went on to become one of the founding members of the Bristol & Wessex Aeroplane Club in 1927, after a brief commission in the Royal Flying Corps between 1926 and 1927. It is possible (but no more than that) that he worked on developing ES & A Robinson's contribution to the Second World War effort - an aircraft template reproduction process which was adopted by almost the whole of the British aircraft industry.

James married comparatively late, in September 1950, having at some point left Bristol, although we don't know when. Working for Robinson's may have been a factor - the company had a ground breaking paper sacks factory at Northfleet, which may have led to James Inskip's acquaintance with Kent - but this is pure speculation.[*]

We don't know much about Pamela - apart from the fact she was forty when she married James (he was forty-nine) and that she was described as an antiques trader when she travelled by trans-Atlantic liner to New York in the 1950s. For most of their residence, Pamela's mother, Olive Mason, lived with them at Higham Hall, together with an Elizabeth Munn, who could have been friend, companion or some kind of domestic help (the latter seems most likely given that later descriptions of the house in this period refer to a staff flat on the top floor - suggesting that at least one member of staff lived in).

We do know the Inskips were proud of the history of their

---

[*]   Coincidentally, my father worked for the same company in the 1960s

house in Higham. Father Andrew Davis, who grew up in Higham and is now retired and living in London, relayed his memories of Higham to me and described how he walked the Inskip's dog and used to help as a 'guide' on open days at Higham Hall and the Farm, showing people the historic barn (from the outside), and various features in the garden, such as the bee boles (see pages 32 and 58 above). Following an article in the Kent Archaeological Society Journal listing local beeboles,[224] the Inskips wrote to the editor to report

'Mr and Mrs Inskip of Higham Hall Rochester have six recesses on their property. Two of these six are of average measurements: 12' to 17' by 28' by 9', face east, have rounded roof arches and are situated in part of the original sixteenth wall of the house. They are undoubtedly bee boles. The remaining four recesses are very large and are of various measurements. It is probable that they, also, are bee boles, but if so they must have housed two skeps. Two of them have a depth of 9', but the remaining two are only 4' in depth, but in this latter case there are signs of infilling. The aspect of two of these four recesses is north, an aspect seldom found in bee boles, and the last two face east and west. The walls are of red brick. Mr Anthony Dale, Investigator of the Ministry of Housing and Local Government assesses the walls as older than the house and puts the date at sixteenth to seventeenth century' [225]

Max Batchelor, a young neighbour of theirs at the time related how when he had only recently passed his driving test, James Inskip wrote to his father, Roy, complaining that Max was driving u p and down Taylors Lane much too fast. Max's reaction was to want to call round to Higham Hall to 'give him a mouthful' but his father more wisely counselled him to write a nice polite letter of apology, which Max did, and neighbourly peace was restored. Max also remembered Pamela as being heavily involved in Guiding, which was another interest that she shared with Beatrice, and some of the older Higham residents remember Girl Guide functions held at Higham Hall during the period that the Inskips lived there.

In 1968, after fourteen years residence, the Inskips put the house up for sale. Advertised in The Times on 24 May, it was described as

> *'A beautiful combination of house and garden, scheduled as of historic and architectural interest, with well laid out walled gardens in first class order, of about 1 acre, including unique collection of rare and choice plants. Outstanding features are the fine walls of Tudor brick, 10-12 feet high, incorporating bee boles and well furnished with fruit, shrubs and climbers; wrought iron gates; Venetian octagonal well head…*
>
> *Ground floor comprises entrance hall, cloakroom, 3 reception rooms, including drawing room with large open hearth and china recess.*
>
> *4-5 bedrooms, 2 bathrooms, 1 en-suite*
>
> *Second floor, 3 rooms and bathroom, suitable as staff flat.*
>
> *Fully automatic central heating'*

Having not sold in the spring, the house was re-advertised in October, with the staff flat described instead as three bedrooms, and at a price of £21,000 to £23,000 (around £460,000 today). This advert also contained some suggestions as to the history of the house - but neither appear to be accurate from what we now know.

'...in Kent near Rochester, is Higham Hall, a basically fifteenth-century building which was re-fronted in regency times after a fire. It is reputedly originally to have been connected with the Benedictine Abbey of Lillechurch, the foundations of which are a mile or so away.'

Once the house had sold, the Inskips moved to Richmond in London. James died in 1977 and Pamela in 2003, aged ninety-three.

Chapter 14

A middle-class home in the late twentieth century

Sometime in 1968/9, the house was bought and occupied by the Smithers family, who again had moved down from London (Westminster and then Dulwich) to take advantage of a more rural lifestyle. Andrew Waldron Smithers (born in 1937) and his wife Amanda moved in with their two sons, Matthew and Jonathan (Kit), then aged four and one. Andrew was the Chairman of Whatman, Reeve, Angel Plc - an investment company. His father was an eminent radiologist who lived in Kent and had a noted fondness for Dickens - perhaps how the Smithers family came upon the house.

Like the Inskips, Amanda had live-in help - the 1970 electoral register records June Sproston in residence with the family. In her advert for a 'mother's help' in the Times in February 1970, Amanda refers to the 'own room and bath' on the top floor. Matthew Smithers has since told me that these rooms were even more self-contained than they are now - while the large room now has two doors, to allow access (and escape) by either staircase, originally when they moved there, the 'servants' part of the top floor could only be accessed by the back stairs. This additional door was put in for fire safety reasons, but the two areas were still kept fairly separate, with the au pair living in the 'servants' half and the boys using the large attic room as a play/games room.

The Smithers' also added the swimming pool, and the changing and pump room, which remained (just!) intact in our day. In all probability they built the existing timber framed garage on the South East corner of the site, although it is a little unclear from subsequent land transfers how the land they owned then extended to the current site of the garage.

Fig 23: Aerial photograph taken in the 1970s

While the Smithers were living at Higham Hall, severe storms blew down one of the garden walls, and reconstruction of this was a significant expense for the owners - given that the brick walls were all ten-feet high and ran the entire length of the large garden. Unsurprisingly, this led to subsequent insurance difficulties and may have contributed to the Smithers' decision to sell the house in 1980 and move back to London. Matthew

(Pelham) Smithers refers to his time there as

> *'For a boy growing up (I lived there from four to fifteen) it was a great place to play, from cycling round the farming estate to escaping to the attic... The garden is where most of the memories lie - the giant mulberry tree in the back garden provided us with copious mulberries for sorbet for many a year - whilst the rose garden to the front right was always a wonder late in the summer.'*

Unfortunately, the mulberry tree had gone by the time we lived there, but we did do some work to re-instate the rose garden, removing some small interloping bushes and shrubs and replanting new roses in their place.

So, having lived there for some twelve years, the Smithers family put Higham Hall up for sale in 1980: it was advertised on 6 June at £150,000, and described as having three reception rooms and a study, four large bedrooms, three small bedrooms, three bathrooms and a games room. A reference to the house being 'surrounded by orchards' suggest that the replacement of the orchards by arable fields that we see in Higham today had not yet taken place. The advertisement explained that Andrew Smithers was spending too much time abroad to take proper advantage of the house, and goes on to describe it as *'a beautiful mansion... believed to date from medieval times...'* before referring to Pevsner's description of the house as *'an eighteenth-century rarity, a genteel house quite unaware of symmetry'*. [226]

From 1981, the house was owned by the Speyer family - Richard and Elizabeth in their late thirties/early forties, and the two daughters, Victoria (then eight) and Sophie (six). They lived there until 1986, moving to Bath with the girls then being thirteen and eleven. The increase in the price of the house - this time advertised at £280,000 - shows the degree of house price inflation in the 1980s.[227] The Speyers appear to have made some minor changes - removing the original front doorway in the middle of the house (which had evolved into a garden door two centuries before) and adding a cupboard in its place). Possibly they also created a dressing room from part of one of the bedrooms, and in the process moved the main bedroom door from its location since Victorian times.

A couple named Alan and Sylvia Holyoake bought the house at some point in 1986, but advertised the house for sale again in October 1988 - listing the house at £550,000 and as having four principal bedrooms - the master with ensuite and dressing room, three to four secondary bedrooms, two further bathrooms, three reception rooms, a study, games room and garden room (the old servants hall). It also lists a summer house, suggesting that they erected the brick structure by the pool. The advert described the well as fourteenth century - but I am not sure on what basis this assertion was made.

Throughout 1989 Higham Hall remained empty and unsold - perhaps it was a little overpriced even for this period of soaring house prices, but it might also have been adversely affected by building work which was being done on the neighbouring farm buildings (which itself may have contributed to the Holyoake's decision to sell). As has been said, in 1988, Guy Batchelor sold the barns and stables which used to belong to Higham Hall and which his family had owned for thirty-eight years, to a property company. Reserving one of Higham Hall cottages to himself, and retaining access to the cold store at the back of the land, Guy thus enabled the creation of the very attractive Ostlers Court development, which has provided homes on the Higham Hall estate for another five families - which has to be the best use of redundant agricultural buildings. Sympathetically converted, this development has allowed the original medieval barn to become a family home, whilst still serving as a living example of a traditional old barn and its place in an ancient farmstead.

Interestingly the plans of the land from 1988 show that not only was the group of roads clustered around Lake Drive not built at this date, the old Higham Hall drive was clearly still visible as a track across the fields from Stedman Close to the garden at the side of the house.

The next owner of Higham Hall was a local businessman, David Fuller. Having bought the house for around £435,000 in March 1990, David lived there with his fiancée, Alison Waack, from 1990 to late 1993. David made some more alterations to the house - he elaborated the second floor games room (the old nursery) by strengthening the floor and adding a snooker table with an overhead light. The cupboard leading off from the drawing room was (apparently) used to house a parrot. They had intended to make improvements to the outdoor space - planning permission was granted for a quadruple garage in the South east corner of the plot - where the existing wooden garage is - but this was never built. They also put up a greenhouse - although the next owners had to take this down on moving in as it had no planning permission - and turned the outdoor summerhouse into a bar.

When David sold up in 1993/4, Philip and Deirdre (Deedle) Catmur moved in with their three young sons - Fergus, Henry and Hugo (aged four, two and two months). Deirdre Catmur's parents, David and Deirdre Clarabut already lived in the area (in 'Trotwood', Dickens Close in Higham) - local knowledge presumably prompting the Catmur's purchase. Despite their short tenure (they sold the house again fourteen months later - Deedle told me that they found it too expensive to run), they had time to make a few alterations - thankfully they replaced a piece of rather ugly concrete rendering at the rear of the house (outside the first floor bathroom) with Kent peg tiles, which certainly must have improved the look of the back of the house. They also sold a small piece of land at the end of the rose garden, which had an old garage built upon it, to the owners of 1 Higham Hall Cottages. The garage dated from the immediate post war period, being erected by the Inskips, who had bought the land from Roy Batchelor.

The pond and its garden were created sometime between the Catmurs moving out in 1995 and 2010 when we bought the house; Deedle Catmur recalled the pond and garage area being a lot more open to the Batchelor's farmland than it is now. The next owners, Terence and Jane Symes, lived in the house with their two sons, Andrew (sixteen) and Paul (fifteen), from 1995 to 2003. They bought the house in March 1995 for 1.3m. Like subsequent owners, they put in planning proposals to build a garage at the rear of the land, but do not appear to have taken it forward. In 2003, British Gas were granted an easement to allow their pipes across the land by the back gate - presumably to supply the new houses in the old farm buildings.

In 2003, the Symes moved to a house in Cooling - their sons were now aged twenty-four and twenty-three, and like us, they may have found Higham Hall a bit large for just two people!

The same year Higham Hall was bought by Matthew Stock (the director of a steel company) and his wife Christina (a teacher). They had three children, Isobel, Emily and Hugh. In 2005, Matthew and Christina bought an additional small piece of land by the gate, presumably to provide room to develop the garage. However, in 2007, they applied for planning permission to build a detached double garage and rear workshop, with a hobbies and games room, in the area of the rose garden, as well as railings each side of the entrance gate. Fortunately for the roses, this was refused. Their plans then turned to the south east corner, and after numerous applications, obtained permission in April 2010. The Stocks did considerable work on the interior of the house, replacing the kitchens and bathrooms. Wanting another project, they moved to the Old Palace, Wrotham.

Thus, when we bought the house from Matthew and Christina Stock on 9 September 2010, planning permission for a rebuilt and redeveloped garage was in place, but we did not pursue it - not least because of the archaeological surveying work which was required (quite rightly) as a condition of permission. We paid £1.45m, for Higham Hall and a year after we moved in, we undertook remedial work to the brickwork on the tower. Two years later, we had the rose garden wall repointed and the coping repaired on both sides. In the course of this, we noticed a small cement plaque in the base of the wall - commemorating 'Juno', who appears to have been a pet - a dog or perhaps a pony. My assumption, in the absence of any more details, was that this was an animal of Dorothy's, since her father would not have found it difficult to obtain a slab of concrete and have the name carved upon it for her as a memorial.

In 2007, Martin and Susan Sutherland who live in one of the old Farm Cottages opposite, bought a small field across from Higham Hall from the Batchelors - I have always assumed that this was the site of Pond Orchard which recurs in a number of the old documents, as there is a small and ancient pond in one corner. The field had been the site of the granary in the 1840s. It also contains the cess pool for the western half of the house - a lingering reminder that the house was once united with the land.

We sold the house in 2015, with some regret, but with the intention of downsizing as we were contemplating retirement and wanted to spend less time running and maintaining a large house and very large garden. We were very pleased to be able to sell the house to a local family - then with two children, now with three. It was very pleasant to think of the house and garden again being home to a growing family, and we hoped they would be as happy there as we were, and many different families before them.

Chapter 15

House history and what it tells us

'So the dilemma confronts us in all its nakedness: if you write local history badly, you are the dreariest of all bores; and if you write it well... it is a pity you can't find something better to do.'

'History... is 'about chaps' and local history brings us nearer to the common run of chaps than any other branch of historical study. ...It studies them as social beings, as members of a rural or urban community; but by seeking them at their home address, it enables us to see them as flesh and blood and not just pawns on the national chessboard.' [228]

These two quotes sum up the difficulties of writing local history - whether that be of house, family or area. Who will want to read it, apart from those to whom it is local? What contribution will it make to the sum total of historical knowledge? Certainly, when I started out on this task, it was simply a desire to know who had lived in and shaped our then home. Anyone who knows Higham will recognise that far from being a rather ordinary commuter village for Gravesend or the Medway Towns; it had a twelfth-century priory and was the site of a ferry crossing over the Thames, before the river was embanked and widened. It has a history. How did our house fit with that?

As other house histories, both in print and on television, have shown, however, there is much truth in Finsberg's second statement. History, on any scale, local, national or international, is made up of individuals. It has been a long time since history was limited to the doings of Kings, Queens and Politicians. Studies in economic and social history have for many years focused on the medieval village, the impact of the Tudor Poor Laws, the Agricultural Revolution, to take a few examples. Studies like these have often been based on detailed local research.

The history of one house in one village can only demonstrate or confirm economic or social trends. Quite obviously, the evidence is too small to be used to draw original conclusions. Just because the seventeenth-century builder of Higham Hall wanted a country home does not mean this was a widespread trend. Neither does the fact that a purchaser in the 1950s split the house and the land prove that all small estates were being broken up. The evidence for these broader trends comes from research and scholarship which has considered many more examples. The value of local history is to provide examples of these nationwide trends - in this case, the comparatively early development of the Londoner's weekend home, and the difficulty of maintaining the traditional small-scale farm in the twentieth century. Without this very real evidence from local conditions, the economic and social historians' arguments are just assertions.

What this small-scale local history also does is to put a human face to those trends. It demonstrates through individuals such as Henry and James Taylor how the complexities of land law, and its peculiarities in Kent, might bite upon the unwary in an age even more litigious than our own. It shows how the tragically common experience of shell shock impacted upon a man like Adam Thorburn and on his family.

In my research, I did not expect to find the people of national significance that I did. We have Eleanor Cordwell, whose comfortable Middlesex upbringing in a prominent 'Roundhead' political family seems worlds away from Taylors Lane in Higham. Her father in law, Samuel Cordwell held a post of importance directly from King Charles II and made an undoubted contribution to the progress of the Civil War. Gerard van Heythuysen collected valuable paintings and exhibited them alongside the founder of the National Gallery. Vitale de Michele, the younger son of a diplomat, made a valuable contribution to the cement and railway industries.

Throughout the course of these researches I have been struck by the way history is made up of a whole chain of smaller transactions. Samuel Cordwell became a gunpowder manufacturer because his patron was in a position to offer him the monopoly on behalf of the King. He seems to have lived in Higham because his father was friendly with another cloth merchant in London. Vitale's father decided to invest in cement as his newspaper and diplomatic careers drew to a close - this led to his son leaving a promising career in railway engineering and making his contribution to the development of the cement industry in North Kent - coupled with his valuable assistance to the work of the Rochester Bridge Trust. They are small individual stories, but join up to contribute to the supply of gunpowder during the English Civil War, and to the development of the Blue Circle cement company - the largest in the world during the 1970s.

If the stories of these people - and perhaps particularly those of Adam and Michael Thorburn - are now more widely known to people in Higham, then this short book has achieved something of value. The final word should go to a contemporary historian, Suzannah Lipscomb. Writing in History Today (December 2019) she notes that

> 'Individual lives do not encompass all history, but despite their messiness, obscurity and fictions, individual lives are the stitches of the past. There would be no fabric of history without them and sometimes we can only really feel the past one thread at a time.' [229]

Endnotes

Introduction

1   'At Home: A Short History of Private Life': Bill Bryson (2010)
2   Great Expectations : Charles Dickens, Penguin edition (1965) p35
3   A History of Higham, Volume II: Andrew Rootes (2012)
4 · 'My father as I recall him': Mary Dickens, Roxburghe Press (1896)
5   'Waterloo Sunset' Ray Davies (1967)

Chapter 1

5   A New and Complete History of the County of Kent: W H Ireland (reprinted 1919)
6   The South East to AD 1000: Peter Drewett, David Rudling, Mark Gardiner (1988), p23
7   A F Allen in Archaeologica Cantiana vol 68, (1954) p144
8   History of Gravesend and its Surroundings: Alex J Philip (1910)
9   English Heritage Rapid Coastal Zone Assessment Reports: North Kent Coast phase ii, Year2, 2005 (pub March 2006)
10 The History and Topographical Survey of the County of Kent, vol 3,: Edward Hasted (1797) pp 481-498
11 Archaeologica Cantiana,. Vol 13, (1880) p494,
12 English Heritage ,op.cit, paragraph 5.1.13
13 'Springhead: An archaeologists dream'; www.wessexarch.co.uk, January 2012
14 R Hiscock places this as a following a line through Denton to Echo Square, then along Cross Lane. 'Essays in Kentish History - The Road between Dartford, Gravesend and Strood' : Archaeologica Cantiana (1968)
15 Historic Desk based Assessment: Cliffe Pools RSPB Reserve: Richard James (2007) Archaeology South East
16 Drewett et al : op cit, p203
17 Ibid, p254
18 Ibid, p319
19 Ibid, p275
20 Essays in Kentish History - Some Fields and Farms in medieval Kent : ARH Baker (1965)
21 The South East from AD1000': Peter Brandon and Brian Short (1990), p8
22 English Heritage, op cit
23 'Historic Farm Buildings': Jeremy Lake, National Trust, (1989) Chapter 2
24   randon and Short, op cit, p 195
25 http://shakespeare.mit.edu/1henryiv/full.html, Act 2, Scene II
26 'A perambulation of Kent; Containing the Description, Historie and Customes of that Shyre': W Lambarde (1567) (rep 1970) pp 6-7
27 'London and north West Kent in the Later Middle Ages: the development of a land

market ': Ann Brown Archaeologica cantium vol 92 1976, p145.

28 Lambarde, p6

29 'The Self Contained Village: the social history of rural communities ' : ed Christopher Dyer, Introduction p3

30 From 'Pehr Kalm's Account of his visit to England': ed J Lucas (1892); quoted in Brandon and Short, p209

31 Brandon amd Short, op cit, p330

32 Rural Rides : William Cobbett (1820), both writers are quoted in Brandon and Short, pp350-1

33 Brandon and Short, op.cit p368

Chapter 2

34 'A History of Higham, Volume I': Andrew Rootes (2011)

35 Historic England, Source ID 1096338

36 'A Handbook of Higham, or the Curiosities of a Country Parish' : Rev. CH Fielding MA (1882), p42.

37 Founding Charter in 'Cartulary of Colchester Abbey, vol 1' : Rt Hon Earl Cooper KG (1897) ed. S Moore, Roxburgh Club

38 Ibid.

39 David Crouch: 'The Reign of King Stephen, 1135-1154', p260

40 [5] Dr Judith Everard: 'The abbey of St Sulpice la Foret and its estates in England 1150-1259', p33

41 ibid

42 A F Davis ' The priory of Higham in Kent: context, history and charters from foundation to dissolution with particular reference to the documents relating to the priory in the archive of St Johns' College Cambridge.' M Phil thesis (2006) University of London, Kings College.

43 This was studied in depth by Fr Andrew Davis in the course of his MPhil thesis (see note 43) and I am indebted to him for sight of this unpublished work

44 ibid p108-9

45 SJCC Archive : Special Collections - D46.27 & D46.58

46 This is consistent with other evidence of land management in Kent - see FRH de Boulay (1959), although Gatty contradicts this in his notes on the archive - see Account of the Finances of the College of St John the Evangelist in the University of Cambridge, 1511-1926: H F Howard (1935).

47 SJCC Archive : D97.250

48 Davis, op cit p69

49 ibid p74

50 ibid

51 'A History of Higham, vol II': Andrew Rootes, 2012, pp 48-50

52 National Archives C3/222/46 Burston v Manwood - Interestingly this Chancery case gave rise to the principle that breach of promise is more significant in contract law than breach of duty. This case continued to be cited in legal textbooks as recently as the 1970s and 1980s.

53 Hasted, op cit (Chapter1)

54 See in particular 'Shorne : the history of a Kentish Village' A F Allen, 1987

55 ibid p 14

56 William Farrar Collection on Honours & Knights Fees: The Homour of Eudo the Steward. MS 711, University of Manchester Library.

57 Subsidy Records, 1242, transcribed for Kent Archaeological Society by Colin Flight, published as British Archaeological Records, British Series 506 (2010)

58 MALSC : Darnley Collection : U565/T119, 122-3 & U565/E134

Chapter 3

59 Will of Samuel Levinge, PROB11/765/530, National Archives

60 Parish Records of St Katharine by the Tower, London. www.ParishRegister.co.uk

61 C2/Jas1/01/10 1616 (Debt due to Estate of Oliver Lycett). National Archives

62 'Alumni Oxonienses 1500-1714': ed Joseph Foster (1891)

63 'The King's Servants: The Civil Service of Charles I 1625-1642' G E Aylmer (1961)

64 Taxation Records - E 115/111/28 & E 115/112/77 National Archives

65 Parish Records of St Andrews Holborn, London. www.ParishRegister.co.uk

66 Luke Cordwell of Higham Esq to Miss Eleanor Roberts (sister of Sir William Roberts of Willesden, Baronet) Marriage Settlement of lands in Kent and elsewhere. 10 November 1664. Lancashire Archives, DDGE (E) 35

67 PROB11/124ff 406r2

68 PROB11/126ff 298v2

69 Registrum Roffensis transcribed by John Thorpe, 1769.

70 Eleanor Roberts' Marriage Settlement, note 67

71 'Kent Clocks & Clockmakers': Michael Pearson (1977). Mayfield Books.

72 Hasted op cit, chapter 1, note 6

73 Historyofparliamentonline.org.uk Thomas Fane (d.1607) of Burston, Hunton Kent

74 PROB11/203/249

75 Brandon and Short, op cit, p195, taken from C Chalklin, '17th century Kent: an economic and social history' (1965)

76 'The Rebuilding of Rural England', W G Hoskins, (November 1953), Past & Present vol 4 Issue 1

77 'Old Houses and Cottages of Kent ': R J Brown (1994)

78 'Domestic Metalwork 1640-1820' : R Gentle & RFeild, Antique Collectors Club (1994) p 332 (Armada Fireback) & p326 (andirons)

79 Historic England, Source ID 1096338

80 V F Desborough Archaeologica Cantiana, vol 70 (1956) p2377.

81 London Faculty Office Marriage Licences.

82 Machen v Waters 1640 - Abstract in 'The Court of Chivalry 1634-40 ed Richard Cust & Andrew Hopper' from British History Online. This was a case where Richard Machen 'whose family has been gentry for up to 100 years' brought proceedings for libel against John Waters 'who was of inferior plebeian stock'. Richard had reprimanded Waters for beating the village constable, provoking a torrent of abuse from Waters, which included the charge that Richard Machen was 'a base shitten gentleman; the Court found for Richard Machen and awarded him £40 in libel damages and £20 in costs.

83 'Saltpeter: The Mother of Gunpowder' David Cressy (2013) p62

Chapter 4

84 [2] Ibid - pp43-44

85 See 'Serving God and Mammon: William Juxton 1582-1663, Bishop of London' Thomas Mason 1944

86 'Highways & Byways of Surrey': Eric Parker, Chapter 10, 'The Villages of the Tillingbourne'.

87 'Activities of Chilworth Mills' Alan Crocker in The Gunpowder Mill Study Group Newsletter (23 August 1998)

88 'The early Stuarts' : Godfrey Davis, Oxford History of England (1959)

89 'A Calendar of the Court Minutes of the East India Company 1635-39' Ethel Bruce Sainsbury (1907), p97

90 Ibid p167

91 'The Cordwell Family: Gunpowder Producers at Chilworth, 1636-1650' : K R Fairclough - Surrey Archaeological Collections 87 (2000) p114

92 'Foedera, conventiones, literae et cujuscunque generis acta publica, inter reges angliae', 1735

93 Whitlocke papers, Vol 8, Ref S/M 1640-2

94 Fairclough op cit p117

95 Alternatively, the reversion may have come through a recommendation from Cordwell's family - the actual holders of this office during the 16th and 17th centuries were the Gyll family of Faversham (gunpowder makers in the 1570's). In 1596, a Robert Cordwell (possibly a relation of Samuel) married Bennett Gyll, and it is possible the Cordwell/Gylls thus recommended Samuel as a suitable future holder of the office. 'Gunpowder Producers as Zookeepers' K R Fairclough, Gunpowder Mills Study Group Newsletters, No 23

96 Aylmer, op cit p280

97 Fairclough note 9, p116

98 Cressy, op cit, p 117

99 Quoted in 'Justice & Petition- The House of Lords & the Refomation of Justice' JS Hart

100 Fairclough note 9, p123

101 Brandon and Short, op cit, p147

102 National Archives - Civil proceedings of the committee for the advancement of money 1642-56

103 National Archives PROB11/203/249

104 Gunpowder & Explosives History group Newsletter 2 February 2001

105 'Curious Bedfellows: Gunpowder Production at Temple Mills Leyton in the early 1650's': Keith Fairclough (2001)

Chapter 5

106 Cordwell v Sanders National Archives C5/27/24 1656; Cordwell v Sanders NA C7/437/40 1647; and C7/85/97 1651

107 Cordell v Cordell (sic) National Archives C5/599/66 1655: Whitelocke papers Vol VIII Ref S/M 1640-42 for Whitelocke's links with Vane

108 'Alumni Oxonienses 1500-1714': ed Joseph Foster (1891)

109 Lancashire County Archives DDGE(E)35Luke Cordwell of Higham Esquire to Miss Eleanor Roberts (sister of Sir William Roberts of at Willesden Baronet); Marriage Settlement of lands in Kent and elsewhere. 10 November 1664

110 Kent Local History Centre Archives U47/12/T18

111 Hearth Tax : Kent Hearth Tax Lady Day 1664 Kent Archaeological Society ed Duncan Harrington Kent Record Society vol XXIX Susan Rose

112 Brandon and Short, op cit, p157

113 Ibid p180

114 'The Diary of Celia Fiennes'; published as 'On a side saddle in the time of William and Mary', by the Hon. Mrs Griffiths (1888)

115 Bockland v Cordwell National Archives C6/386/87 1682

116 http://aalt.law.uh.edu/Attorneys/attpages/Attorneys1607.html

117 Dictionary of National Biography

118 http://innertemplearchives.org.uk/

119 National Archives PROB11/765/530 22 November 1748

120 From papers in the West Sussex Record Office, SAS-S 239, 249 & 258

121 Ibid, SAS/A477-480

122 Papers in the East Sussex Record Office, SAS/A473A

Chapter 6

123 'Elizabeth's London': Lisa Picard (2003)

124 www.ancestry.co.uk

125 'Dictionary of National Biography' : Sarah Palmer

126 'Immigrants of Note'; London Historians Blog : Mike Patterson

127 www.nationalgallery.org.uk/collectorsandbenefactors

Chapter 7

128 'The Medieval English Economy 1150-1500': J L Bolton, p26

129 'A History of Farm Buildings in England & Wales' : Nigel Harvey (1984) pp64-5

130 Ibid p72

131 Kent Local History Centre Archives: U47/T205

132 ibid

133 Ibid

134 ibid

135 ibid

136 ibid

137 Medway Archives and Local Studies Centre Archives: Parish Record Book - Higham with Murston : P185/8/1

138 Ibid (note 4)

139 Ibid

140 ibid

141 Land Tax Records

142 Ibid (note 4)

143 Reports of Cases argued and determined in the English courts of Common Law : ed Thomas Sergeant, Vol 32 (1837)

Chapter 8

144 Medway Archives and Local Studies Centre : Parish Records : Higham with Merston

145 'Fruit Growing in Kent in the 19th Century' : D Harvey (1964). The production of apples benefitted particularly form the coming of the railways as they were more robust than other fruits and therefore easy to transport by rail.

146 A History of Higham, Volume I': Andrew Rootes, p20

147 Essex Herald, Tuesday March 23, 1841

148 Kent Archaeological Society : Memorial Inscriptions : D E William (2012), from Leland Duncan's notebooks

149 'Shops and Shopkeeping in 18th Century England' : Hon Chueng Miu & Lorna H Mui : quoted in http://London-city-historiography-.org.uk

Chapter 9

150 Op cit

151 Quoted in http://London-city-historiography-.org.uk

152 This description and those following come from sale particulars published by J Shuttleworth for the 1843 auction. These are located in the Archives of St Johns College Cambridge at D.97.329, and I am indebted to the then archivist Malcolm G Underwood who found and sent them on to me.

Chapter 10

153 All of the letters and diaries used in this chapter and the next are held by the Bodleian Library, in their Special collections section, in folios 671, 682, 683, 686 and 886. They are unsorted but clearly were once considered worthy of publication - various references to money and some of the less polite comments about individuals have been struck through with a red pencil.

154 Folio 682

155 Folio 683, doc 136, 13 November 1858

156 Folio 683, docs 141, 143 & 145

157 Folio 683, docs 163, 168 & 171

158 Folio 886, doc 9

159 'The Cement Industry 1796-1914: A History' A J Francis (1977) p168

160 Ibid p171

161 www.kent.gov.uk/exploringKent'spast

162 www.cementkilns.co.uk/cement_kiln_cliffe_creek.html

163 Victorian Cliffe http://www.kentrigs.org.uk/cliffepools/htm . Description of the works by Vitale de Michele quoted in the report of the Inquiry into the Collision between the Steamships Capulet and Hapsburg on 4 March 1881

164 Daily News, 2 December 1874

165 Francis, op cit, pp 172-3

166 Archives of the Rochester Bridge Trust, Correspondence file.

167 Folio 683, doc 73

168 Folio 886, doc 60

169 [17] ' Higham In Old Photographs' A Rootes & S Williams (2004) p35

170 'Gilbert of Gilbert & Sullivan: His Life & Character' Andrew Crowther (2011) p139

171 Folio 886

172 Folio 886 doc 32

173 Deeds relating to the purchase which are currently in my possession

174 Folio 686, doc 74

175 Folio 686, docs 172-4

176 Folio 686 doc 76

177 Folio 683 docs, 99, 108 & 117

178 Folio 683, doc 87

179 Both from Folio 683, doc 93

180 Folio 683, doc 83

181 Folio 886

182 Archives of the Rochester Bridge, Minute Books

183 SE Gazette, May 5 & April 7 1896 and 18 October 1898 and Kent Local History Centre Archives, Higham School Log Book, CKS C/ES 185/1/1 1897-1925

184 'Isle of Grain Railways: Adrian Gray': The wharf itself at Cliffe remained in use for the loading of clay until the 1960's. Quoted in Cement Kilns: Victorian Cliffe, on the Cliffe at Hoo Historical Society website.

185 'Higham's Historic Houses': Davis Barnes (2003), published in 'The Bridge', Higham Parish magazine, pp6-7

186 'R W Schultz: an Arts and Crafts Architect: David Ottewill, in Architectural History, v22, pp87-115 (1979)

187 Folio 886

188 Folio 886, doc 46

189 Folio 886, doc 42

190 37 Folio 886, doc 47

191 Inland Revenue Land Valuations 6 April 1909, IR4/57/1

Chapter 11

192 Folio 886

193 Folio 686, doc 141

194 Folio 686, docs 143-4

195 Southern Reporter, 8 August 1907

196 From the WI History of Higham, quoted in 'A History of Higham, vol 1 ': Andrew Rootes, p28

197 Folio 886, doc 63

198 www.thelonglongtrail.co.uk C Baker 'Researching soldiers of the British Army in the War of 1914-18: The Battle of Loos'

199 Folio 685

200 Folio 685

201 Folio 685

202 Folio 685

203 A History of Higham, Vol 1: Andrew Rootes, p 50

204 Folio 686, doc 77

205 Folio 686, doc 176

206 Folio 686, doc 167

207 Folio 686, doc 181

208 Folio 686, doc 183
209 Folio 686, doc 184
210 Brighton PRO 6562

Chapter 12

211 'Higham in Old Photographs' Compiled by Andrew Rootes and Sue Williams, A
     Higham Village History Group project 2004, p57
212 From Kathleen Gay's obituary in the Journal of Psychic Research, written by Ro-
     salind Hayward, vol 49, 1977-8.
213 The Dundee Courier, October 2 1922 (BNA)
214 London Gazette, 1 January 1918
215 Kent & Sussex Courier, January 23 1923 (BNA)
216 The Pall Mall Gazette, January 15 1923 (BNA)
217 Fruit Growing in Kent in the 19th century': David Harvey, Archaeologica Cantium,
     vol 79, 1964, p95ff
218 Northants Evening Telegraph, 13 October 1939
219 National Farm Survey 1941-43 MAF/32/1027/257
220 ibid
221 'A History of Higham, Volume 1' : Andrew Rootes,. p77

Chapter 13

222 The Times 31 October 1949
223 Gravesend Reporter 24 October 1975
224 V Desborough Archaeologica cantiae vol 69, 1956
225 Letters AC vol 70 1956, pp239-40

Chapter 14

226 Chatham News 6 June 1980
227 Chatham Rochester and Gillingham News 15 August 1986]
228 'The Local Historian and his Theme' H P R Finsberg Dept of English Local History
     Occasional Papers no. 1, University College of Leicester 6 November 1952. Pub-
     lished by Leicester University press (1965)

Chapter 15

229 'Gossiping with the Dead': Susannah Lipscomb, in History Today (December
     2019), Vol 69 Issue 12

Appendices

Appendix 1

An Inventory

Of the household furniture, plate, linen, china and other effects belonging to the late Mr John Taylor in the parish of Higham appraised to Mr Henry Taylor, the 2nd day of January 1796

No. 1 Garrett

A stump bedstead, feather bed and bolster, 3 blankets, a quilt and a pair of sheets, a chair, a bowl

No 2 Men's Room

A four poster bedstead, a feather bed and bolster, 3 blankets, a jug, a pair of sheets, a chair, an old jack

No 3 Green Room

A four poster bedstead with Green damask furniture, a feather bed and bolster, 3 blankets, a pair of sheets, a quilt, a mahogany bureau, a wainscot dressing table, a square box dressing glass, 2 prints in black and gold frames, 2 brown stuff window curtains, laths [shutters] and linen

No 4 Back Room adjoining

A four poster tent bedstead with striped cotton furniture, a flock mattress, a feather bed bolster, and one pillow, four blankets, a pair of sheets, a white cotton counterpane, 2 cherry tree chairs, a square dressing glass

No5 passage

15 paintings various subjects

No 6 Front Room

6 mahogany chairs with crimson damask loose seats with cotton covers, 2 elbow chairs, a brass fronted stove and brass fender and set of fire irons, an oval mahogany dining table, a card table, 3 green worsted damask window curtains, a pier glass [mirror]in walnut tree frame, a small Wilton carpet, 3 side carpets, 3 prints, 8 wine glasses, 2 rummers [glasses], one tumbler, 5 blue and white china plates (2 cracked), 1 blue and white tea pot (cracked), a blue and white tea pot and stand, a blue and white tea canister, milk pot, sugar basin and cover, 6 coffee cups, 5 tea cups, 1 saucer, a sugar basin, 2 silver tablespoons, 5 teaspoons, a pair of silver sugar tongs, 12 plated handle dessert spoons, silver table knives and forks, 6 green handle dessert spoons, silver ferril [ferrule], 2 silver salts, a silver pepper caster, 5 books, 5 coarse sheets, a piece of [cloth] prepared for sewing.

No 7 Little Parlour

6 mahogany chairs, a yew tree arm chair, a pier glass in mahogany frame, 6 paintings in gilt frames, a weather glass, a ladder back stool, copper coal scuttle, a brass fronted stove with blower and brass fender

No 8 Hall

A mahogany pillar table, a mahogany oval dining table, a green arm chair, a green stool, 2 clothes horses, a high back arm chair, 2 yards stair carpet with iron rods

No 9 Kitchen

A small kitchen range, an iron bar, 3 pot hooks, a poker, shovel and tongs, a trivet, a small copper, tea kettle, a copper as fixed in brickwork, a small brass pointed jack [spit], a copper can, a copper coffee pot, 2 brass candlesticks, 2 iron candlesticks, a flat iron, a pair of snuffers, a 30 hour clock, an old wainscot table, a copper frying pan, a copper saucepan, a small saucepan and a pair of copper scales, 4 pewter dishes, 16 pewter plates, a dutch oven, a pail

No 10 Room adjoining

A kneading trough, a small pair of grators

No 11 Dairy

A bottle jack as fixed, 10 dozen of wine & beer bottles, a churn, a stick, a milk pail, 3 butter prints, a small wood bowl, a Hog board

No12 Wash-house

1 brewing copper fixed in brickwork with large cock [tap], a malt mill, a washing copper fixed in brick work, 2 brewing tubs, a parcel of sundries

No 13 Garden

An old lead cistern, a stone bowl, a dove house, a hen house

The whole of the household furniture and other effects

belonging to the late Mr John Taylor at Higham are valued and appraised at ninety pounds, sixteen shillings and six pence, the 2nd day of January 1796.

County of Kent

Particulars

Of the

Higham Hall Estate

An Extensive and Peculiarly Valuable

FREEHOLD LANDED PROPERTY

Most desirably situate in and around the pleasing village
of Higham within the compass of a mile and a half of the
Falstaff hotel, Gads hill about four miles from Gravesend
and three from Rochester

In a rich district of the

County of Kent

Intersected by the

Thames and Medway Canal

Which for the conveyance of Fruit, Agricultural produce
and manure, offers singular advantages for horticultural and
Farming operations; - comprising altogether

154 a 0r 22p

Disposed in highly productive orchards, market gardens,
detached lands, Dwelling houses and cottages, with numerous sites for building on the North and elevated side of
the Thames

The present low rental

£662:2:0 per annum

Which will be sold by auction by Messrs

Shuttleworth and Sons

At the Mart opposite the Bank of England

On Friday June 23 1843 at Twelve o'clock in twenty six lots

PARTICULARS

THIS VERY DESIRABLE ESTATE

Comprising the Relics of the Ancient Celebrated Mansion of
HIGHAM HALL, converted into Farming Residences, with
several Cottages, Buildings and

about

ONE HUNDRED AND FIFTY FOUR ACRES

Of very superior land, chiefly cultivated as Fruit and
Vegetable Gardens for the supply of the London Markets,
but producing also excellent crops of wheat, barley, peas,
beans, potatoes, rye grass, clover and other seeds; and lying
in numerous detached inclosures, pieces and parcels, fronting upon good roads; the major part presenting beautiful
sites of building, commanding extensive and picturesque
prospects over the meanders of the Thames and Medway and
all the rich country adjacent, with facilities for travelling by
coach and steam nearly every hour throughout the day

The Property is at present occupied by most respectable
tenants chiefly on lease or agreements for leases for short

periods now to run and offers advantageous opportunities for investment with which view it has been arranged for sale in numerous attractive lots within the range of moderate capitalists.

Lot 1   A freehold estate situate at TWO GATES in the parish of Higham, comprising a commodious Cottage containing 2 bedchambers, 2 parlours, a wash house and oven with a packing shed adjoining and an inclosure of Market Garden Ground, planted with numerous fruit trees and inclosed by a neat quick hedge, the whole containing two acres and thirty one perches. *In the occupation of Mr John Lindridge at a net rent of £18 per annum.*

Lot 2 A freehold estate situate at Two Gates, opposite Lot 1, called THE DASTY HILL, comprising ten acres, three roods, and fourteen perches, of Arable Land, Garden Ground, and Orcharding, with a barn and shed erected thereon. *In the occupation of Mr John Lindridge at a net rent of £35, 10s per annum.*

Lot 3 A freehold estate situate between CHURCH STREET LANE, Higham and Brick House, the residence of William Stunt, Esq. comprising two pieces of superior Arable Land, containing together eighteen acres, three roods and thirty four perches, being formerly parts and parcels of the Ancient Common Fields of Higham. *In the occupation of William Barnes at a net rent of £55 per annum*

Lot 4 A freehold estate adjoining the last mentioned Lot, comprising three pieces of superior Arable Land, containing together eight acres, one rood and nineteen perches. *In* the occupation of Mr William Stunt, at a net rent of £12 5s per annum

Lot 5 A freehold estate situate near the Chequers Public House in the VILLAGE of Higham. Consisting of a Double Cottage or Tenement containing Six Rooms with appurtenances and a Garden in the rear, containing altogether twenty one perches. *In the occupation of Allen Thatcher at a net rent of £10 per annum*

Lot 6 situate adjoining Lot 5 and comprising THE MALT SHOVEL BEER SHOP, formerly the Parish Workhouse, containing three Garretts, five sleeping rooms, a Tap Room, Parlour, kitchen, wash house and cellaring with a yard and large and well stocked garden in the rear, containing in the whole, two roods and thirteen perches. *In the occupation of Thomas Pett at a net rent of £23 per annum*

Lot 7 situate in the village of Higham, adjoining the preceding Lot, consisting of an inclosure of Rich Arable Land comprising one acre, two roods and thirty three perches. *In the occupation of William Easdown at a net rent of £7 per annum*

Lot 8 situate in the village of Higham, a short distance from the previous Lots, consisting of a Large Double Cottage or Tenement, containing 5 rooms with cart lodges, stable, and other Outbuildings, and a large well stocked garden, the whole comprising three roods and four perches. *Part in the occupation of Mrs Mary Hompstead at £8 per annum and part in the occupation of Mr Joseph Hearn at £8 8s*

Lot 9 Situate near Lot 8 but in the Parish of Chalk, a Fine

Young Orchard and Market Garden, comprising one acre, one rood, and thirty six perches. *In the occupation of Mrs Hompstead at a net rent of £10 per annum*

Lot 10 situate opposite Lot 9 but in the Parish of Higham, a Fine Young Orchard and Market Garden, comprising one acre, one rood and seventeen perches. *In the occupation of Mrs Hompstead at a net rent of £8 per annum*

Lot 11 situate in Higham near Lot 10, a piece of superior Arable Land, comprising three acres, one rood and thirty five perches. *In the occupation of Mrs Hompstead at a net rent of £12 19s per annum*

Lot 12 situate opposite Higham Hall consisting of a piece of superior Arable land, comprising two acres, one rood and twenty eight perches. *In the occupation of Mr William Barnes at a net rent of £7 per annum*

Lot 13 situate partly adjoining Lot 12 and opposite Higham Hall consisting of a piece of Arable Land and Orcharding, comprising three acres, one rood and twelve perches, with a Timber built Granary on Stone Staddles, placed thereon. *In the occupation of Mr William Barnes at a net rent of £15 per annum*

Lot 14 comprising Higham Hall House. Commanding an elevated and very agreeable situation, adapted for a moderate sized family and containing, three attics, four family bed chambers, two neat parlours, a kitchen, scullery and pantry, a large court yard, brew house with loft over, stable. Chaise house, and excellent walled garden very abundantly stocked with productive fruit trees and outer garden or shrubbery, and plantation. A farm yard, team stable for five horses, barn cart lodge, and granary. Also two very fine orchards, meadow land and rich market garden ground. The whole comprising six acres and twenty nine perches. Also two commonings in Higham Common Fields. *One Commoning is let to Mr William Stunt at a net rent of £1 8s 6d. Part of the Filbert orchard, and the part of the 6 acre field is let to Mr William Easdown jnr, at a net rent of £21 per annum. The other part of the premises is let to Mr William Barnes at a net rent of £62 10s per annum*

Lot 15 situate adjoining to the preceeding consisting of a Neat Brick Dwelling House, containing two bedchambers, a parlour, kitchen and washhouse with a stable for four horses and loft over, shed, yard, and small garden, with a malt house, granary and cart lodge. Also a market garden, orchard and Arable field, the whole comprising ten acres and twelve perches. And 1 commoning in Higham Common Field. *In the occupation of Mr William Easdown Jnr at a net rent of £84 per annum and the communing is let to Mr William Stunt at a net rent of £1 8s and 6d.*

Lot 16 situate opposite Lot 15 consisting of three pieces of superior Arable land, containing together eleven acres and nine perches. *In the occupation of Mr William Barnes at a net rent of £32 2s per annum*

Lot 17 situate a short distance from Lot 16 consisting of four pieces of superior Arable land, containing together fourteen acres, two roods and thirty three perches. *In the occupation of Mr William Barnes at a net rent of £53 1s* *per annum*

Lot 18 situate nearly opposite Lot 17 consisting of one piece of superior Arable land, comprising eight acres, one rood and nine perches. *In the occupation of Mr William Barnes at a net rent of £25 per annum*

Lot 19 situate nearly opposite to Lot 18 consisting of four pieces of superior Young Orchard, Market Garden Ground and Arable land, with a substantial double cottage erected thereon, containing four bedrooms, two sitting rooms, two kitchens and cellaring. Also a stable, cart lodge and shed. Containing together sixteen acres, two roods and twenty eight perches. *In the occupation of Mr William Barnes at a net rent of £87 10s per annum*

Lot 20 situate nearly opposite Lot 19 consisting of one piece of superior Arable land, containing one acre and twenty nine perches. *In the occupation of Mr William Barnes at a net rent of £3 10s per annum*

Lot 21 situate a short distance from the preceding Lots, consisting of a fine Young Orchard and Market Garden containing three acres, three roods and twenty seven perches. *In the occupation of Mr George Brooks at a net rent of £14 per annum*

Lot 22 situate near the preceding Lot, consisting of a fine Young Orchard, Market Garden and Wood Lands, one piece planted with Oaks containing altogether four acres, two roods and eighteen perches. *Part is in the occupation of Mr Thomas Youens at a net rent of £15 per annum. The rest is in the occupation of Mr William Barnes at a net rent of £1* *per annum*

Lot 23 situate opposite the preceding Lots, consisting of a piece of superior Arable Land containing two acres and four perches. *In the occupation of Mr William Easdown Snr at a net rent of £4 per annum*

Lot 24 situate in CHURCH STREET LANE Higham, adjoining Mr Easadown's house, called The Hoblitts, comprising five acres, one rood and eight perches of fine Young Orcharding and Market Garden ground. *In the occupation of Mr William Easdown at a net rent of £17 per annum*

Lot 25 situate near the CHEQUERS at Higham, consisting of one piece of Arable Land containing one acre, two roods and thirty four perches. *In the occupation of Mr Lake at a net rent of £5 per annum*

Lot 26 situate in the Marshes of the Parish of Higham, near Higham Creek, consisting of thirteen pieces of marsh or saltings, comprising together eleven acres and thirty five perches. *In the occupation of Mr George Brooks at a net rent of £14 per annum*

Appendix 3

Chatham, Rochester and Gillingham News

Friday March 28th 1924, page 5

Fire at Higham Hall

Major and his Household's Fierce Fight with Flames

Higham Hall, the charming old Elizabethan mansion, situated at some distance from the railway station, was the scene of a disastrous fire, on Saturday morning. At 6.30 or thereabouts, the cook, who sleeps on the top storey, was awakened by a strong smell of burning, and upon investigation, she discovered that the box-room, also on the top floor, was alight. She immediately called her master, Major Thorburn, who was sleeping underneath in a room on the second storey.

Luckily the bailiff and other workers on the estate were close at hand and heard the Major's call for assistance. After some difficulty, they managed to fix a hosepipe to the bathroom tap, and after a furious fight with the flames, succeeded in keeping the conflagration more or less in hand until the fire brigade came to their assistance. Meanwhile, the Major and a few neighbours carried out the furniture and effects, amongst which were several valuable pictures and carved woodwork.

In a short space of time, the Rochester Fire brigade, under Chief Officer H Webb, arrived and soon completely extinguished the flames. The Brigade are to be congratulated on the prompt and determined manner in which they worked for, according to an eye-witness, the box-room was a veritable furnace. Apart from the structural damage done by the fire, the great flow of water caused a fair amount of havoc in the rooms immediately underneath; books, pictures and furniture being completely ruined, whilst the house itself is not considered safe to live in, the ceiling and walls being in a state of collapse. Fortunately, nothing of great value was kept in the box-room although several furs and a considerable amount of clothing was destroyed by the flames.

So far as he is able to judge, by the state of the rooms, Major Thorburn estimates the amount of damage done to value of £1000.*

Mrs and Miss Thorburn, who were in another wing of the house suffering from an attack of the measles, were severely upset by the catastrophe, and have had to be removed to the bailiff's house.

When interviewed by a 'News' reporter, Major Thorburn stated that although he had commanded a battalion in the war, he did not think he has ever fought so fiercely before. 'I fought like a tiger 'he said 'and I think our escape is perfectly miraculous.' The Major spoke in eulogistic terms of the great assistance rendered by the employees and remarked that if it had not been for them, as well as for the promptitude of the Rochester Fire Brigade, the house would have been completely destroyed. Happily, no-one was at all hurt by the flames, although Major Thorburn had his night attire considerably burned. The Major intimated his intention of leaving the house as soon as possible, as it was not habitable in its present condition.

* £1000 is worth around £47,000 in today's money.

Appendix 4

The varying size of the estate in sale particulars:

1781	150 acres	This included land in Chalk, Cliffe, Shorne and Frindsbury, bought by Richard Machen, and held together until the time of Samuel Levinge
1834	64 acres	Bought by James Taylor from his brother, John Henry Taylor. Other land may have been retained by John Henry or sold off separately
1841	70 acres	Rented by William Barnes and forming the core of the estate
1851	110	Rented by William Barnes, and showing the addition of neighbouring land
1859	55 acres	Reflecting the break up of the land-holding into more saleable units by Edward Eagleton
1928-1950	74-78 acres	The core part of the estate, owned by the Thorburns, and eventually sold as farmland to the Batchelors

List of Figures :

Bibliography

Primary Sources

C2/Jas1/01/10 1616 (Debt due to Estate of Oliver Lycett). The National Archives (TNA)

C3/222/46 Burston v Manwood TNA

C5/27/24 Cordwell v Sanders 1656 TNA; C7/437/40 Cordwell v Sanders 1647 TNA ; and C7/85/97 Cordwell v Sanders 1651 TNA

C5/599/66 Cordell v Cordell (sic) 1655 TNA

C6/386/87 1682 Bockland v Cordwell TNA

SP46/80 fo 248 Payments (Navy & Custome Cttee) TNA

Civil proceedings of the committee for the advancement of money 1642-56 TNA

Inland Revenue Land Valuations TNA

National Farm Survey 1941-43 MAF/32/1027/257 TNA

Taxation Records - E 115/111/28 & E 115/112/77 TNA

Will of Thomas Machen PROB11/124/671, TNA

Will of Christian Machen PROB11/126/432, TNA

Will of Edmund Cordwell PROB11/141/24

Will of Samuel Cordwell PROB11/203/249 TNA

Will of Mary Cordwell PROB11/359/92 TNA

Will of Samuel Levinge PROB11/765/530 TNA

Probate Records, Principal registry London: Wills of Vitale de Michele, Beatrice de Michele, Dorothy Thorburn, Beatrice Thorburn

Oxford Bodleian Library, Special collections MS Eng Lett c. 671, 682, 683, 686 and 886. De Michele family papers.

St Johns College Cambridge Archive : Special Collections - D46.27, D46.58, D97.250, D.97.329. Papers relating to Higham and Higham Priory.

Luke Cordwell of Higham Esq to Miss Eleanor Roberts (sister of Sir William Roberts of Willesden, Baronet) Marriage Settlement of lands in Kent and elsewhere. 10 November 1664. Lancashire Archives, DDGE (E) 35

Kent Local History Centre Archives: Title Deeds U47/12/T18, U47/1/T205, U47/22 T70, 161; Land Tax duplicates Q/RPI/178

Deeds relating to Higham Hall which are currently in my possession

Archives of the Rochester Bridge Trust, Correspondence file.

Archives of the Rochester Bridge, Minute Books

Medway Archives and Local Studies Collection : Darnley Collection : U565/T119 &

L14, 122-3 & U565/E134; Parish Record Book - Higham with Murston P185/8/1, PCC Minutes 1740-1857 ; Strood Rural District Council Papers SRDC/BP/1870; 583, War Damage Books; Higham School Log Book, CKS C/ES 185/1/1 1897-1925;

East Sussex Record Office, SAS/A473A. Papers relating to Howe Court

West Sussex Record Office, SAS-S 239, 249 & 258, SAS/A477-480. Papers relating to Howe Court

Printed Sources

'Foedera, conventiones, literae et cujuscunque generis acta publica, inter reges angliae'

Kelly' Directory of the Medway Towns, various editions

Bagshaw's Directory - various

Post Office Directory - various

Melville's Directory - various

Electoral Registers for Strood Rural District Council, Medway Rural District Council, Gravesham Borough Council

Reports of Cases argued and determined in the English courts of Common Law : ed Thomas Sergeant, Vol 32 (1837)

Registrum Roffensis transcribed by John Thorpe, 1769

Abstracts of Probate Acts: The Perogative Court of Canterbury. Volume IV Anno 1648.

Whitelocke papers Vol VIII Ref S/M

Historic England, Source ID 1096338

'Alumni Oxonienses 1500-1714': ed Joseph Foster (1891)

English Heritage Rapid Coastal Zone Reports: North Kent Coast Phase ii, Year 2, 2005 (March 2006)

Kent Archaeological Society : Memorial Inscriptions : D E William (2012), from Leland Duncan's notebooks

Subsidy Records, 1242, transcribed for Kent Archaeological Society by Colin Flight, published as British Archaeological Records, British Series 506 (2010)

William Farrar Collection on Honours & Knights Fees: The Honour of Eudo the Steward. MS 711, University of Manchester Library.

'Cartulary of Colchester Abbey, vol 1': Rt Hon Earl Cooper KG (1897) ed. S Moore

'Kent Hearth Tax Lady Day 1664': Susan Rose , Kent Archaeological Society ed Duncan Harrington Kent Record Society vol XXIX

'A Calendar of the Court Minutes of the East India Company 1635-39' Ethel Bruce Sainsbury (1907)

Newspapers

Essex Herald, 23 March, 1841

The London Standard, 10 May 1843

Edinburgh Gazette, 29 August 1856

Daily News, 23 May 1864 & 25 April 1865

Daily News, 2 December 1874

London Gazette, 29 April 1890

Morning Post, 28 April 1893

SE Gazette, 7 April & 5 May 1896 and 18 October 1898

Chatham Observer, 24 March 1906

Southern Reporter, 8 August 1907

London Gazette, 1 January 1918

The Dundee Courier, 2 October 1922 (British Newspaper Archive BNA)

Kent & Sussex Courier, 23 January 1923 (BNA)

The Pall Mall Gazette, 15 January 1923 (BNA)

Kent & Sussex Courier, 23 January 1923 (BNA)

Berwickshire News, 14 June 1926

The Scotsman, 14 December 1931

The Times, 19 August 1934

The Scotsman, 4 December 1934

Northants Evening Telegraph, 13 October 1939

The Times, 31 October 1949

Gravesend Reporter, 24 October 1975

Chatham News, January 1980

Chatham Rochester and Gillingham News 15 August 1986

Irish Review 1988

Secondary Sources

Articles

'Higham's Historic Houses': Davis Barnes (2003), published in 'The Bridge', Higham Parish magazine

'Late Continued Demesne Farming in Otford': F R H du Boulay, Archaeologia Cantiana vol 73 (1959)

'Activities of Chilworth Mills' Alan Crocker in The Gunpowder Mill Study Group Newsletter (23 August 1998)

'Bee Boles and Beehouses': V F Desborough Archaeologia Cantiana vol 69, (1956)

'Further Bee Boles in Kent': V F Desborough Archaeologia Cantiana, vol 70 (1956)

Letters Archaeologica Cantiana vol 70 1956,

'The Abbey of St Sulpice La Foret and Royal Patronage in England c1150-1259': Dr Judith Everard, Nottingham Medieval Studies, vol XLVII (2003)

'Curious Bedfellows: Gunpowder Production at Temple Mills Leyton in the early 1650's': Keith Fairclough (2001)

'The Cordwell Family: Gunpowder Producers at Chilworth, 1636-1650' : K R Fairclough - Surrey Archaeological Collections 87 (2000)

'Chilworth Gunpowder Mills in the period of the Dutch Wars': K R Fairclough and Glenys Crocker - Surrey Archaeological Collections, 92 (2005)

'The East India Company and Gunpowder Production in England 1624 - 1636': K R Fairclough, Surrey Archaeological Collections 87 (2000)

'Gunpowder Producers as Zookeepers' K R Fairclough, Gunpowder Mills Study Group Newsletters, No 23

'The Local Historian and his Theme' H P R Finsberg Dept of English Local History Occasional Papers no. 1, University College of Leicester 6 November 1952. Published by Leicester University press (1965)

'Fruit Growing in Kent in the 19th Century': D Harvey Archaeologia Cantiana 79 (1964)

Journal of Psychic Research, Obituary of Kathleen Gay, written by Rosalind Hayward, vol 49, 1977-8

'The Road between Dartford, Gravesend and Strood' Essays in Kentish History: R Hiscox, Archaeologia Cantiana (1968)

'The Rebuilding of Rural England', W G Hoskins, Past & Present vol 4 Issue 1 (November 1953)

'R W Schultz: an Arts and Crafts Architect: David Ottewill, in Architectural History, v22, pp87-115 (1979)

'Ancient Iron Firebacks': John Parsons, Journal of Kentish History, Vol 4, 1977

'Josiah Dewye and the Carshalton Gun Mills': M Wilks, Gunpowder Mills Study Group Newsletter 8 (1990)

Books

'Shorne : the history of a Kentish Village' A F Allen (1987)

'The King's Servants: The Civil Service of Charles I 1625-1642' G E Aylmer (1961)

'The Medieval English Economy 1150-1500': J L Bolton (1980)

'Charles the First': John Bowle (1975)

'The South East from AD 1000: Longman's Regional History of England': Peter Brandon and Brian Short (1990)

'Old Houses and Cottages of Kent ': R J Brown (1994)

'Brick building in Britain': R W Brunskill (1990)

'Saltpeter: The Mother of Gunpowder' David Cressy (2013)

'The Reign of King Stephen, 1135-1154': David Crouch (2000)

'Gilbert of Gilbert & Sullivan: His Life & Character' Andrew Crowther (2011)

'The Early Stuarts' : Godfrey Davis, Oxford History of England (1959)

'Great Expectations': Charles Dickens (1965)

'My father as I recall him': Mary Dickens (1896)

'The South East to AD1000. Longman Regional History of England:' Peter Drewett, David Rudling, Mark Gardiner (1988)

'The Self-Contained Village - The Social History of Rural Communities 1250-1900': Christopher Dyer (2006)

'Dealing in Death: The Arms Trade and the British Civil Wars 1638-52': Peter Edwards (2000)

'A Handbook of Higham, or the Curiosities of a Country Parish': Rev. CH Fielding MA (1882)

'The Cement Industry 1796-1914: A History' A J Francis (1977)

'Domestic Metalwork 1640-1820' : R Gentle & R Feild, Antique Collectors Club (1994)

'The Diary of Celia Fiennes'; published as 'On a side saddle in the time of William and Mary', by the Hon. Mrs Griffiths (1888)

'Justice Upon Petition' - the House of Lords and the Reformation of Justice 1621-1675' JS Hart (1991)

'A History of Farm Buildings in England & Wales' : Nigel Harvey (1984)

'The History and Topographical Survey of the County of Kent' Edward Hasted (1797)

'The English Fireplace: Its Architecture and the Working Fire': Nicholas Hills (1983)

'Account of the Finances of the College of St John the Evangelist in the University of Cambridge, 1511-1926': H F Howard (1935)

'English Houses 1300-1800': Matthew Johnson (2010)

'Historic Farm Buildings': Jeremy Lake (1989)

'A Perambulation of Kent': William Lambarde (1576)

'Serving God and Mammon: William Juxton 1582-1663, Bishop of London' Thomas Mason (1944)

'Vishnu's Crowded Temple: India since the Great Rebellion': Maria Misra (2007)

'Shops and Shopkeeping in 18th Century England' : Hon Chueng Miu & Lorna H Mui (1999)

'The Dutch in London 1580-1800; the influence of an immigrant community': David Ormorod (1973)

'Highways & Byways of Surrey': Eric Parker (1935)

'Kent Clocks & Clockmakers': Michael Pearson (1977)

'History of Gravesend & it's Surroundings': A J Philip (1910)

'Elizabeth's London': Lisa Picard (2003)

'A History of Higham, Volume I': Andrew Rootes (2011)

'A History of Higham, Volume II': Andrew Rootes (2012)

Higham In Old Photographs' A Rootes & S Williams (2004)

'A Life of John Julius Angerstein, 1735-1823: widening circles in finance, philanthropy and the arts in eighteenth century London.': Anthony Twist (2006)

Websites

http://aalt.law.uh.edu/Attorneys/attpages/Attorneys1607.html

www.ancestry.co.uk Census records 1841-1911

www.bgas.org.uk Transactions, Volume 64 'Machen Family History': H A Machen (1943)

https://www.bmj.com

*https://www.**british-history**.ac.uk* 'The Court of Chivalry 1634-40' ed Richard Cust & Andrew Hopper. Machen v Waters 1640

www.cementkilns.co.uk/cement_kiln_cliffe_creek.html

www.cems.ox.ac.uk Francis Lodwick Biographical details

https://www.historychristchurch.org.uk *Highcliffe Castle*

http://www.cliffehistory.co.uk/ 'Isle of Grain Railways: Adrian Gray': Cement Kilns: Victorian Cliffe

www.clockmakers.org Clockmaker's Company Website

https://www.oxforddnb.com Dictionary of National Biography

www.fretwell.kangaweb.com.au/pdfs/EmilyKitson.pdf

Historyofparliamentonline.org.uk Thomas Fane (d.1607) of Burston, Hunton

www.ice.org.uk Institute of Civil Engineers

http://innertemplearchives.org.uk/

www.kent.gov.uk/exploringKent'spast

http://www.kentrigs.org.uk/cliffepools/htm

http://London-city-historiography-.org.uk 'Immigrants of Note'; London Historians Blog : Mike Patterson

www.thelonglongtrail.co.uk C Baker 'Researching soldiers of the British Army in the War of 1914-18: The Battle of Loos'

www.nationalgallery.org.uk/collectorsandbenefactors

www.ParishRegister.co.uk Parish Records of St Katharine by the Tower, London, Parish Records of St Andrews Holborn, London

http://shakespeare.mit.edu/1henryiv/full.html, Act 2, Scene II

www.uboat.net/allies/warships/ship/4288

Unpublished Material

'The priory of Higham in Kent: context, history and charters from foundation to dissolution with particular reference to the documents relating to the priory in the archive of St Johns' College Cambridge.' M Phil thesis A F Davis 2006 University of London, Kings College

Letter from Jenny Kauntze, Records Archivist at FANY (March 2012)